fedora

Fedora 11
Security-Enhanced Linux
User Guide

Fultus[TM] *Books*

Fedora 11
Security-Enhanced Linux User Guide

ISBN 1-59682-145-0

Copyright © 2009 Red Hat, Inc. and others. All rights reserved.

Cover design and book layout by Fultus Corporation

Published by Fultus Corporation

Publisher Web: *www.fultus.com*
Linbrary - Linux Library: *www.linbrary.com*
Online Bookstore: *store.fultus.com*
email: *production@fultus.com*

This material may only be distributed subject to the terms and conditions set forth in the Open Publication License, V1.0, (the latest version is presently available at *http://www.opencontent.org/openpub/*).

Fedora and the Fedora Infinity Design logo are trademarks or registered trademarks of Red Hat, Inc., in the U.S. and other countries. Red Hat and the Red Hat "Shadow Man" logo are registered trademarks of Red Hat Inc. in the United States and other countries. All product names and services identified throughout this manual are trademarks or registered trademarks of their respective companies.

The author and publisher have made every effort in the preparation of this book to ensure the accuracy of the information. However, the information contained in this book is offered without warranty, either express or implied. Neither the author nor the publisher nor any dealer or distributor will be held liable for any damages caused or alleged to be caused either directly or indirectly by this book.

fedora

Fediora Release	Book Name	Edition
F11	Security-Enhanced Linux User Guide	1.3

Authors	Emails
Murray McAllister Red Hat Engineering Content Services	*mmcallis@redhat.com*
Daniel Walsh Red Hat Security Engineering	*dwalsh@redhat.com*
Dominick Grift Technical editor for the Introduction, SELinux Contexts, Targeted Policy, Working with SELinux, Confining Users, and Troubleshooting chapters.	*domg472@gmail.com*
Eric Paris Technical editor for the Mounting File Systems and Raw Audit Messages sections. Red Hat Security Engineering	*eparis@parisplace.org*
James Morris Technical editor for the Introduction and Targeted Policy chapters. Red Hat Security Engineering	*jmorris@redhat.com*
Scott Radvan Red Hat Engineering Content Services	*sradvan@redhat.com*

Copyright © 2009 Red Hat, Inc.

Table of Contents

Legal Notice

Copyright © 2009 Red Hat, Inc. This material may only be distributed subject to the terms and conditions set forth in the Open Publication License, V1.0, (the latest version is presently available at *http://www.opencontent.org/openpub/*).

Fedora and the Fedora Infinity Design logo are trademarks or registered trademarks of Red Hat, Inc., in the U.S. and other countries.

Red Hat and the Red Hat "Shadow Man" logo are registered trademarks of Red Hat Inc. in the United States and other countries.

All other trademarks and copyrights referred to are the property of their respective owners.

Documentation, as with software itself, may be subject to export control. Read about Fedora Project export controls at *http://fedoraproject.org/wiki/Legal/Export*.

Abstract

This book is about managing and using Security-Enhanced Linux®.

Preface

The Fedora 11 SELinux User Guide is for people with minimal or no experience with SELinux. Although system administration experience is not necessary, content in this guide is written for system administration tasks. This guide provides an introduction to fundamental concepts and practical applications of SELinux. After reading this guide you should have an intermediate understanding of SELinux.

Thank you to everyone who offered encouragement, help, and testing - it is most appreciated. Very special thanks to:

- Dominick Grift, Stephen Smalley, and Russell Coker for their contributions, help, and patience.
- Karsten Wade for his help, adding a component for this guide to *Red Hat Bugzilla*[1], and sorting out web hosting on *http://docs.fedoraproject.org/*.
- The *Fedora Infrastructure Team*[2] for providing hosting.
- Jens-Ulrik Petersen for making sure the Red Hat Brisbane office has up-to-date Fedora mirrors.

1. Document Conventions

This manual uses several conventions to highlight certain words and phrases and draw attention to specific pieces of information.

In PDF and paper editions, this manual uses typefaces drawn from the *Liberation Fonts*[3] set. The Liberation Fonts set is also used in HTML editions if the set is installed on your system. If not, alternative but equivalent typefaces are displayed. Note: Red Hat Enterprise Linux 5 and later includes the Liberation Fonts set by default.

1.1. Typographic Conventions

Four typographic conventions are used to call attention to specific words and phrases. These conventions, and the circumstances they apply to, are as follows.

---

[1] *https://bugzilla.redhat.com/*
[2] *http://fedoraproject.org/wiki/Infrastructure*
[3] *https://fedorahosted.org/liberation-fonts/*

`Mono-spaced Bold`

Used to highlight system input, including shell commands, file names and paths. Also used to highlight key caps and key-combinations. For example:

> To see the contents of the file `my_next_bestselling_novel` in your current working directory, enter the `cat my_next_bestselling_novel` command at the shell prompt and press **Enter** to execute the command.

The above includes a file name, a shell command and a key cap, all presented in Mono-spaced Bold and all distinguishable thanks to context.

Key-combinations can be distinguished from key caps by the hyphen connecting each part of a key-combination. For example:

> Press **Enter** to execute the command.

> Press **Ctrl+Alt+F1** to switch to the first virtual terminal. Press **Ctrl+Alt+F7** to return to your X-Windows session.

The first sentence highlights the particular key cap to press. The second highlights two sets of three key caps, each set pressed simultaneously.

If source code is discussed, class names, methods, functions, variable names and returned values mentioned within a paragraph will be presented as above, in `Mono-spaced Bold`. For example:

> File-related classes include `filesystem` for file systems, `file` for files, and `dir` for directories. Each class has its own associated set of permissions.

Proportional Bold

This denotes words or phrases encountered on a system, including application names; dialogue box text; labelled buttons; check-box and radio button labels; menu titles and sub-menu titles. For example:

> Choose **System > Preferences > Mouse** from the main menu bar to launch **Mouse Preferences**. In the **Buttons** tab, click the **Left-handed mouse** check box and click **Close** to switch the primary mouse button from the left to the right (making the mouse suitable for use in the left hand).

> To insert a special character into a **gedit** file, choose **Applications > Accessories > Character Map** from the main menu bar. Next, choose **Search > Find…** from the **Character Map** menu bar, type the name of the character in the **Search** field and click **Next**. The character you sought will be highlighted in the **Character Table**. Double-click this highlighted character to place it in the **Text to copy** field and then click the **Copy** button. Now switch back to your document and choose **Edit > Paste** from the **gedit** menu bar.

The above text includes application names; system-wide menu names and items; application-specific menu names; and buttons and text found within a GUI interface, all presented in Proportional Bold and all distinguishable by context.

Note the > shorthand used to indicate traversal through a menu and its sub-menus. This is to avoid the difficult-to-follow 'Select **Mouse** from the **Preferences** sub-menu in the **System** menu of the main menu bar' approach.

`Mono-spaced Bold Italic` or **`Proportional Bold Italic`**

Whether Mono-spaced Bold or Proportional Bold, the addition of Italics indicates replaceable or variable text. Italics denotes text you do not input literally or displayed text that changes depending on circumstance. For example:

To connect to a remote machine using ssh, type `ssh` *`username@domain.name`* at a shell prompt. If the remote machine is `example.com` and your username on that machine is john, type `ssh john@example.com`.

The `mount -o remount` *`file-system`* command remounts the named file system. For example, to remount the `/home` file system, the command is `mount -o remount /home`.

To see the version of a currently installed package, use the `rpm -q` *`package`* command. It will return a result as follows: *`package-version-release`*.

Note the words in bold italics above — username, domain.name, file-system, package, version and release. Each word is a placeholder, either for text you enter when issuing a command or for text displayed by the system.

Aside from standard usage for presenting the title of a work, italics denotes the first use of a new and important term. For example:

When the Apache HTTP Server accepts requests, it dispatches child processes or threads to handle them. This group of child processes or threads is known as a *server-pool*. Under Apache HTTP Server 2.0, the responsibility for creating and maintaining these server-pools has been abstracted to a group of modules called *Multi-Processing Modules* (*MPMs*). Unlike other modules, only one module from the MPM group can be loaded by the Apache HTTP Server.

1.2. Pull-quote Conventions

Two, commonly multi-line, data types are set off visually from the surrounding text.

Output sent to a terminal is set in `Mono-spaced Roman` and presented thus:

```
books          Desktop    documentation   drafts   mss     photos    stuff   svn
books_tests    Desktop1   downloads       images   notes   scripts   svgs
```

Source-code listings are also set in `Mono-spaced Roman` but are presented and highlighted as follows:

```
package org.jboss.book.jca.ex1;

import javax.naming.InitialContext;

public class ExClient
{
   public static void main(String args[])
      throws Exception
   {
      InitialContext iniCtx = new InitialContext();
      Object          ref    = iniCtx.lookup("EchoBean");
      EchoHome        home   = (EchoHome) ref;
      Echo            echo   = home.create();

      System.out.println("Created Echo");

      System.out.println("Echo.echo('Hello') = " + echo.echo("Hello"));
   }

}
```

1.3. Notes and Warnings

Finally, we use three visual styles to draw attention to information that might otherwise be overlooked.

Note

A note is a tip or shortcut or alternative approach to the task at hand. Ignoring a note should have no negative consequences, but you might miss out on a trick that makes your life easier.

Important

Important boxes detail things that are easily missed: configuration changes that only apply to the current session, or services that need restarting before an update will apply. Ignoring Important boxes won't cause data loss but may cause irritation and frustration.

Warning

A Warning should not be ignored. Ignoring warnings will most likely cause data loss.

2. We Need Feedback!

If you find a typographical error in this manual, or if you have thought of a way to make this manual better, we would love to hear from you! Please submit a report in Bugzilla: *http://bugzilla.redhat.com/bugzilla/* against the product **Fedora Documentation.**

When submitting a bug report, be sure to mention the manual's identifier: *selinux-user-guide*

If you have a suggestion for improving the documentation, try to be as specific as possible when describing it. If you have found an error, please include the section number and some of the surrounding text so we can find it easily.

Chapter 1.
Trademark Information

Linux® is the registered trademark of Linus Torvalds in the U.S. and other countries.

UNIX is a registered trademark of The Open Group.

Type Enforcement is a trademark of Secure Computing, LLC, a wholly owned subsidiary of McAfee, Inc., registered in the U.S. and in other countries. Neither McAfee nor Secure Computing, LLC, has consented to the use or reference to this trademark by the author outside of this guide.

Apache is a trademark of The Apache Software Foundation.

MySQL is a trademark or registered trademark of MySQL AB in the U.S. and other countries.

1.1. Source Code

The XML source for this guide is available at *http://svn.fedorahosted.org/svn/selinuxguide/*

Chapter 2.
Introduction

Files, such as directories and devices, are called objects. Processes, such as a user running a command or the Mozilla® Firefox® application, are called subjects. Most operating systems use a Discretionary Access Control (DAC) system that controls how subjects interact with objects, and how subjects interact with each other. On operating systems using DAC, users control the permissions of files (objects) that they own. For example, on Linux® operating systems, users can make their home directories world-readable, giving users and processes (subjects) access to potentially sensitive information.

DAC mechanisms are fundamentally inadequate for strong system security. DAC access decisions are only based on user identity and ownership, ignoring other security-relevant information such as the role of the user, the function and trustworthiness of the program, and the sensitivity and integrity of the data. Each user has complete discretion over their files, making it impossible to enforce a system-wide security policy. Furthermore, every program run by a user inherits all of the permissions granted to the user and is free to change access to the user's files, so no protection is provided against malicious software. Many system services and privileged programs must run with coarse-grained privileges that far exceed their requirements, so that a flaw in any one of these programs can be exploited to obtain complete system access.[1]

The following is an example of permissions used on Linux operating systems that do not run Security-Enhanced Linux (SELinux). The permissions in these examples may differ from your system. Use the `ls -l` command to view file permissions:

```
$ ls -l file1
-rwxrw-r-- 1 user1 group1 0 2009-04-30 15:42 file1
```

The first three permission bits, `rwx`, control the access the Linux `user1` user (in this case, the owner) has to `file1`. The next three permission bits, `rw-`, control the access the Linux

---

[1] "Integrating Flexible Support for Security Policies into the Linux Operating System", by Peter Loscocco and Stephen Smalley. This paper was originally prepared for the National Security Agency and is, consequently, in the public domain. Refer to the *original paper* *<http://www.nsa.gov/research/_files/selinux/papers/freenix01/index.shtml>* for details and the document as it was first released. Any edits and changes were done by Murray McAllister.

`group1` group has to `file1`. The last three permission bits, `r--`, control the access everyone else has to `file1`, which includes all users and processes.

Security-Enhanced Linux (SELinux) adds Mandatory Access Control (MAC) to the Linux kernel, and is enabled by default in Fedora. A general purpose MAC architecture needs the ability to enforce an administratively-set security policy over all processes and files in the system, basing decisions on labels containing a variety of security-relevant information. When properly implemented, it enables a system to adequately defend itself and offers critical support for application security by protecting against the tampering with, and bypassing of, secured applications. MAC provides strong separation of applications that permits the safe execution of untrustworthy applications. Its ability to limit the privileges associated with executing processes limits the scope of potential damage that can result from the exploitation of vulnerabilities in applications and system services. MAC enables information to be protected from legitimate users with limited authorization as well as from authorized users who have unwittingly executed malicious applications.[2]

The following is an example of the labels containing security-relevant information that are used on processes, Linux users, and files, on Linux operating systems that run SELinux. This information is called the SELinux context, and is viewed using the `ls -Z` command:

```
$ ls -Z file1
-rwxrw-r--  user1 group1 unconfined_u:object_r:user_home_t:s0      file1
```

In this example, SELinux provides a user (`unconfined_u`), a role (`object_r`), a type (`user_home_t`), and a level (`s0`). This information is used to make access control decisions. With DAC, access is controlled based only on Linux user and group IDs. SELinux policy rules are checked after DAC rules. SELinux policy rules are not used if DAC rules deny access first.

Linux and SELinux Users

On Linux operating systems that run SELinux, there are Linux users as well as SELinux users. SELinux users are part of SELinux policy. Linux users are mapped to SELinux users. To avoid confusion, this guide uses "Linux user" and "SELinux user" to differentiate between the two.

2.1. Benefits of running SELinux

- All processes and files are labeled with a type. A type defines a domain for processes, and a type for files. Processes are separated from each other by running in

---

[2] "Meeting Critical Security Objectives with Security-Enhanced Linux", by Peter Loscocco and Stephen Smalley. This paper was originally prepared for the National Security Agency and is, consequently, in the public domain. Refer to the *original paper* *<http://www.nsa.gov/research/_files/selinux/papers/ottawa01/index.shtml>* for details and the document as it was first released. Any edits and changes were done by Murray McAllister.

their own domains, and SELinux policy rules define how processes interact with files, as well as how processes interact with each other. Access is only allowed if an SELinux policy rule exists that specifically allows it.

- Fine-grained access control. Stepping beyond traditional UNIX® permissions that are controlled at user discretion and based on Linux user and group IDs, SELinux access decisions are based on all available information, such as an SELinux user, role, type, and, optionally, a level.
- SELinux policy is administratively-defined, enforced system-wide, and is not set at user discretion.
- Reduced vulnerability to privilege escalation attacks. One example: since processes run in domains, and are therefore separated from each other, and SELinux policy rules define how processes access files and other processes, if a process is compromised, the attacker only has access to the normal functions of that process, and to files the process has been configured to have access to. For example, if the Apache HTTP Server is compromised, an attacker can not use that process to read files in user home directories, unless a specific SELinux policy rule was added or configured to allow such access.
- SELinux can be used to enforce data confidentiality and integrity, as well as protecting processes from untrusted inputs.

SELinux is not:

- antivirus software.
- a replacement for passwords, firewalls, or other security systems.
- an all-in-one security solution.

SELinux is designed to enhance existing security solutions, not replace them. Even when running SELinux, continue to follow good security practices, such as keeping software up-to-date, using hard-to-guess passwords, firewalls, and so on.

2.2. Examples

The following examples demonstrate how SELinux increases security:

- the default action is deny. If an SELinux policy rule does not exist to allow access, such as for a process opening a file, access is denied.
- SELinux can confine Linux users. A number of confined SELinux users exist. Linux users can be mapped to SELinux users to take advantage of confined SELinux users. For example, mapping a Linux user to the SELinux user_u user, results in a Linux user that is not able to run (unless configured otherwise) set user ID (setuid) applications, such as `sudo` and `su`, as well as preventing them from executing files and applications in their home directory- if configured, this prevents users from executing malicious files from their home directories.

- process separation. Processes run in their own domains, preventing processes from accessing files used by other processes, as well as processes accessing other processes. For example, when running SELinux, unless otherwise configured, an attacker can not compromise a Samba server, and then use that Samba server to read and write to files used by other processes, such as databases used by MySQL®.
- help limit the damage done by configuration mistakes. *Domain Name System (DNS)*[3] servers can replicate information between each other. This is known as a zone transfer. Attackers can use zone transfers to update DNS servers with false information. When running the *Berkeley Internet Name Domain (BIND)*[4] DNS server in Fedora 11, even if an administrator forgets to limit which servers can perform a zone transfer, the default SELinux policy prevents zone files[5] from being updated by zone transfers, the BIND `named` daemon, and other processes.
- refer to the Red Hat® *Magazine*[6] article, *Risk report: Three years of Red Hat Enterprise Linux 4*[7], for exploits that were restricted due to the default SELinux targeted policy in Red Hat® Enterprise Linux® 4.
- refer to the *LinuxWorld.com*[8] article, *A seatbelt for server software: SELinux blocks real-world exploits*[9], for background information about SELinux, and information about various exploits that SELinux has prevented.
- refer to James Morris's *SELinux mitigates remote root vulnerability in OpenPegasus*[10] blog post, for information about an exploit in *OpenPegasus*[11] that was mitigated by SELinux as shipped with Red Hat Enterprise Linux 4 and 5.

The *Tresys Technology*[12] website has an *SELinux Mitigation News*[13] section (on the right-hand side), that lists recent exploits that have been mitigated or prevented by SELinux.

---

[3] *http://en.wikipedia.org/wiki/Domain_Name_System*

[4] *https://www.isc.org/software/bind*

[5] Text files that include information, such as hostname to IP address mappings, that are used by DNS servers.

[6] *http://www.redhatmagazine.com/*

[7] Cox, Mark. "Risk report: Three years of Red Hat Enterprise Linux 4". Published 26 February 2008. Accessed 28 August 2008: *http://www.redhatmagazine.com/2008/02/26/risk-report-three-years-of-red-hat-enterprise-linux-4/*.

[8] *http://www.linuxworld.com/*

[9] Marti, Don. "A seatbelt for server software: SELinux blocks real-world exploits". Published 24 February 2008. Accessed 28 August 2008: *http://www.linuxworld.com/news/2008/022408-selinux.html?page=1*.

[10] *http://james-morris.livejournal.com/25421.html*

[11] *http://www.openpegasus.org/*

[12] *http://www.tresys.com/*

[13] *http://www.tresys.com/innovation.php*

2.3. SELinux Architecture

SELinux is a Linux security module that is built into the Linux kernel. SELinux is driven by loadable policy rules. When security-relevant access is taking place, such as when a process attempts to open a file, the operation is intercepted in the kernel by SELinux. If an SELinux policy rule allows the operation, it continues, otherwise, the operation is blocked and the process receives an error.

SELinux decisions, such as allowing or disallowing access, are cached. This cache is known as the Access Vector Cache (AVC). Caching decisions decreases how often SELinux policy rules need to be checked, which increases performance. SELinux policy rules have no effect if DAC rules deny access first.

2.4. SELinux on Other Operating Systems

Refer to the following for information about running SELinux on operating systems:

- Hardened Gentoo: *http://www.gentoo.org/proj/en/hardened/selinux/selinux-handbook.xml*.
- Debian: *http://wiki.debian.org/SELinux*.
- Ubuntu: *https://wiki.ubuntu.com/SELinux* and *https://help.ubuntu.com/community/SELinux*.
- Red Hat Enterprise Linux: *Red Hat Enterprise Linux Deployment Guide*[14] and *Red Hat Enterprise Linux 4 SELinux Guide*[15].
- Fedora: *http://fedoraproject.org/wiki/SELinux* and the *Fedora Core 5 SELinux FAQ*[16].

---

[14] *http://www.redhat.com/docs/en-US/Red_Hat_Enterprise_Linux/5.2/html/Deployment_Guide/selg-overview.html*
[15] *http://www.redhat.com/docs/manuals/enterprise/RHEL-4-Manual/selinux-guide/*
[16] *http://docs.fedoraproject.org/selinux-faq-fc5/*

Chapter 3.
SELinux Contexts

Processes and files are labeled with an SELinux context that contains additional information, such as an SELinux user, role, type, and, optionally, a level. When running SELinux, all of this information is used to make access control decisions. In Fedora 11, SELinux provides a combination of Role-Based Access Control (RBAC), Type Enforcement® (TE), and, optionally, Multi-Level Security (MLS).

The following is an example SELinux context. SELinux contexts are used on processes, Linux users, and files, on Linux operating systems that run SELinux. Use the `ls -Z` command to view the SELinux context of files and directories:

```
$ ls -Z file1
-rwxrw-r--  user1 group1 unconfined_u:object_r:user_home_t:s0      file1
```

SELinux contexts follow the *SELinux user:role:type:level* syntax:

SELinux user

The SELinux user identity is an identity known to the policy that is authorized for a specific set of roles, and for a specific MLS range. Each Linux user is mapped to an SELinux user via SELinux policy. This allows Linux users to inherit the restrictions on SELinux users. The mapped SELinux user identity is used in the SELinux context for processes in that session, in order to bound what roles and levels they can enter. Run the `semanage login -l` command as the Linux root user to view a list of mappings between SELinux and Linux user accounts:

```
# /usr/sbin/semanage login -l

Login Name                SELinux User              MLS/MCS Range

__default__               unconfined_u              s0-s0:c0.c1023
root                      unconfined_u              s0-s0:c0.c1023
system_u                  system_u                  s0-s0:c0.c1023
```

Output may differ from system to system. The `Login Name` column lists Linux users, and the the `SELinux User` column lists which SELinux user is mapped to which Linux user. For processes, the SELinux user limits which roles and levels are accessible. The last column, `MLS/MCS Range`, is the level used by Multi-Level Security (MLS) and Multi-Category Security (MCS). Levels are briefly discussed later.

role

Part of SELinux is the Role-Based Access Control (RBAC) security model. The role is an attribute of RBAC. SELinux users are authorized for roles, and roles are authorized for domains. The role serves as an intermediary between domains and SELinux users. The roles that can be entered determine which domains can be entered - ultimately, this controls which object types can be accessed. This helps reduce vulnerability to privilege escalation attacks.

type

The type is an attribute of Type Enforcement. The type defines a domain for processes, and a type for files. SELinux policy rules define how types access each other, whether it be a domain accessing a type, or a domain accessing another domain. Access is only allowed if a specific SELinux policy rule exists that allows it.

level

The level is an attribute of MLS and Multi-Category Security (MCS). An MLS range is a pair of levels, written as *lowlevel-highlevel* if the levels differ, or *lowlevel* if the levels are identical (`s0-s0` is the same as `s0`). Each level is a sensitivity-category pair, with categories being optional. If there are categories, the level is written as *sensitivity:category-set*. If there are no categories, it is written as *sensitivity*.

If the category set is a contiguous series, it can be abbreviated. For example, `c0.c3` is the same as `c0,c1,c2,c3`. The `/etc/selinux/targeted/setrans.conf` file maps levels (`s0:c0`) to human-readable form (`CompanyConfidential`). Do not edit `setrans.conf` with a text editor: use `semanage` to make changes. Refer to the semanage(8) manual page for further information. In Fedora 11, targeted policy enforces MCS, and in MCS, there is one sensitivity, `s0`. MCS in Fedora 11 supports 1024 different categories: `c0` through to `c1023`. `s0-s0:c0.c1023` is sensitivity `s0` and authorized for all categories.

MLS enforces the *Bell-LaPadula Mandatory Access Model*[1], and is used in Labeled Security Protection Profile (LSPP) environments. To use MLS restrictions, install the selinux-policy-mls package, and configure MLS to be the default SELinux policy. The MLS policy shipped with Fedora omits many program domains that were not part of the evaluated configuration, and therefore, MLS on a desktop workstation is unusable (no support for the X Window System); however, an MLS policy from the *upstream SELinux Reference Policy*[2] can be built that includes all program domains.

---

[1] *http://en.wikipedia.org/wiki/Bell-LaPadula_model*
[2] *http://oss.tresys.com/projects/refpolicy*

3.1. Domain Transitions

A process in one domain transitions to another domain by executing an application that has the `entrypoint` type for the new domain. The `entrypoint` permission is used in SELinux policy, and controls which applications can be used to enter a domain. The following example demonstrates a domain transition:

1. A users wants to change their password. To change their password, they run the `passwd` application. The `/usr/bin/passwd` executable is labeled with the `passwd_exec_t` type:

   ```
   $ ls -Z /usr/bin/passwd
   -rwsr-xr-x  root root system_u:object_r:passwd_exec_t:s0 /usr/bin/passwd
   ```

   The **passwd** application accesses `/etc/shadow`, which is labeled with the `shadow_t` type:

   ```
   $ ls -Z /etc/shadow
   -r--------  root root system_u:object_r:shadow_t:s0   /etc/shadow
   ```

2. An SELinux policy rule states that processes running in the `passwd_t` domain are allowed to read and write to files labeled with the `shadow_t` type. The `shadow_t` type is only applied to files that are required for a password change. This includes `/etc/gshadow`, `/etc/shadow`, and their backup files.

3. An SELinux policy rule states that the `passwd_t` domain has `entrypoint` permission to the `passwd_exec_t` type.

4. When a user runs the `/usr/bin/passwd` application, the user's shell process transitions to the `passwd_t` domain. With SELinux, since the default action is to deny, and a rule exists that allows (among other things) applications running in the `passwd_t` domain to access files labeled with the `shadow_t` type, the **passwd** application is allowed to access `/etc/shadow`, and update the user's password.

This example is not exhaustive, and is used as a basic example to explain domain transition. Although there is an actual rule that allows subjects running in the `passwd_t` domain to access objects labeled with the `shadow_t` file type, other SELinux policy rules must be met before the subject can transition to a new domain. In this example, Type Enforcement ensures:

- the `passwd_t` domain can only be entered by executing an application labeled with the `passwd_exec_t` type; can only execute from authorized shared libraries, such as the `lib_t` type; and can not execute any other applications.
- only authorized domains, such as `passwd_t`, can write to files labeled with the `shadow_t` type. Even if other processes are running with superuser privileges, those processes can not write to files labeled with the `shadow_t` type, as they are not running in the `passwd_t` domain.

- only authorized domains can transition to the `passwd_t` domain. For example, the `sendmail` process running in the `sendmail_t` domain does not have a legitimate reason to execute `passwd`; therefore, it can never transition to the `passwd_t` domain.
- processes running in the `passwd_t` domain can only read and write to authorized types, such as files labeled with the `etc_t` or `shadow_t` types. This prevents the **passwd** application from being tricked into reading or writing arbitrary files.

3.2. SELinux Contexts for Processes

Use the `ps -eZ` command to view the SELinux context for processes. For example:

1. Open a terminal, such as **Applications** → **System Tools** → **Terminal**.
2. Run the `/usr/bin/passwd` command. Do not enter a new password.
3. Open a new tab, or another terminal, and run the `ps -eZ | grep passwd` command. The output is similar to the following:

```
unconfined_u:unconfined_r:passwd_t:s0-s0:c0.c1023 13212 pts/1 00:00:00
passwd
```

4. In the first tab, press **Ctrl+C** to cancel the **passwd** application.

In this example, when the `/usr/bin/passwd` application (labeled with the `passwd_exec_t` type) is executed, the user's shell process transitions to the `passwd_t` domain. Remember: the type defines a domain for processes, and a type for files.

Use the `ps -eZ` command to view the SELinux contexts for running processes. The following is a limited example of the output, and may differ on your system:

```
system_u:system_r:setroubleshootd_t:s0 1866 ?   00:00:08 setroubleshootd
system_u:system_r:dhcpc_t:s0         1869 ?        00:00:00 dhclient
system_u:system_r:sshd_t:s0-s0:c0.c1023 1882 ? 00:00:00 sshd
system_u:system_r:gpm_t:s0           1964 ?        00:00:00 gpm
system_u:system_r:crond_t:s0-s0:c0.c1023 1973 ? 00:00:00 crond
system_u:system_r:kerneloops_t:s0 1983 ?         00:00:05 kerneloops
system_u:system_r:crond_t:s0-s0:c0.c1023 1991 ? 00:00:00 atd
```

The `system_r` role is used for system processes, such as daemons. Type Enforcement then separates each domain.

3.3. SELinux Contexts for Users

Use the `id -Z` command to view the SELinux context associated with your Linux user:

```
unconfined_u:unconfined_r:unconfined_t:s0-s0:c0.c1023
```

In Fedora 11, Linux users run unconfined by default. This SELinux context shows that the Linux user is mapped to the SELinux `unconfined_u` user, running as the `unconfined_r` role, and is running in the `unconfined_t` domain. `s0-s0` is an MLS range, which in this case, is the same as just `s0`. The categories the user has access to is defined by `c0.c1023`, which is all categories (`c0` through to `c1023`).

Chapter 4.
Targeted Policy

Targeted policy is the default SELinux policy used in Fedora 11. When using targeted policy, processes that are targeted run in a confined domain, and processes that are not targeted run in an unconfined domain. For example, by default, logged in users run in the `unconfined_t` domain, and system processes started by init run in the `initrc_t` domain - both of these domains are unconfined.

Unconfined domains (as well as confined domains) are subject to executable and writeable memory checks. By default, subjects running in an unconfined domain can not allocate writeable memory and execute it. This reduces vulnerability to *buffer overflow attacks*[1]. These memory checks are disabled by setting Booleans, which allow the SELinux policy to be modified at runtime. Boolean configuration is discussed later.

4.1. Confined Processes

Almost every service that listens on a network is confined in Fedora 11. Also, most processes that run as the Linux root user and perform tasks for users, such as the **passwd** application, are confined. When a process is confined, it runs in its own domain, such as the `httpd` process running in the `httpd_t` domain. If a confined process is compromised by an attacker, depending on SELinux policy configuration, an attacker's access to resources and the possible damage they can do is limited.

The following example demonstrates how SELinux prevents the Apache HTTP Server (`httpd`) from reading files that are not correctly labeled, such as files intended for use by Samba. This is an example, and should not be used in production. It assumes that the httpd, wget, setroubleshoot-server, and audit packages are installed, that the SELinux targeted policy is used, and that SELinux is running in enforcing mode:

1. Run the `sestatus` command to confirm that SELinux is enabled, is running in enforcing mode, and that targeted policy is being used:

   ```
   $ /usr/sbin/sestatus
   ```

---

[1] *http://en.wikipedia.org/wiki/Buffer_overflow*

```
SELinux status:                 enabled
SELinuxfs mount:                /selinux
Current mode:                   enforcing
Mode from config file:          enforcing
Policy version:                 23
Policy from config file:        targeted
```

`SELinux status: enabled` is returned when SELinux is enabled. `Current mode: enforcing` is returned when SELinux is running in enforcing mode. `Policy from config file: targeted` is returned when the SELinux targeted policy is used.

2. As the Linux root user, run the `touch /var/www/html/testfile` command to create a file.

3. Run the `ls -Z /var/www/html/testfile` command to view the SELinux context:

```
-rw-r--r--  root root unconfined_u:object_r:httpd_sys_content_t:s0
/var/www/html/testfile
```

By default, Linux users run unconfined in Fedora 11, which is why the `testfile` file is labeled with the SELinux `unconfined_u` user. RBAC is used for processes, not files. Roles do not have a meaning for files - the `object_r` role is a generic role used for files (on persistent storage and network file systems). Under the `/proc/` directory, files related to processes may use the `system_r` role.[2] The `httpd_sys_content_t` type allows the `httpd` process to access this file.

4. As the Linux root user, run the `service httpd start` command to start the `httpd` process. The output is as follows if `httpd` starts successfully:

```
# /sbin/service httpd start
Starting httpd:                                        [  OK  ]
```

5. Change into a directory where your Linux user has write access to, and run the `wget http://localhost/testfile` command. Unless there are changes to the default configuration, this command succeeds:

```
--2009-05-06 23:00:01--  http://localhost/testfile
Resolving localhost... 127.0.0.1
Connecting to localhost|127.0.0.1|:80... connected.
HTTP request sent, awaiting response... 200 OK
Length: 0 [text/plain]
Saving to: `testfile'

[ <=>                             ] 0       --.-K/s    in 0s

2009-05-06 23:00:01 (0.00 B/s) - `testfile' saved [0/0]
```

6. The `chcon` command relabels files; however, such label changes do not survive when the file system is relabeled. For permanent changes that survive a file system relabel,

---

[2] When using other policies, such as MLS, other roles may be used, for example, `secadm_r`.

use the `semanage` command, which is discussed later. As the Linux root user, run the following command to change the type to a type used by Samba:

```
chcon -t samba_share_t /var/www/html/testfile
```

Run the `ls -Z /var/www/html/testfile` command to view the changes:

```
-rw-r--r--  root root unconfined_u:object_r:samba_share_t:s0
/var/www/html/testfile
```

7. Note: the current DAC permissions allow the `httpd` process access to `testfile`. Change into a directory where your Linux user has write access to, and run the `wget http://localhost/testfile` command. Unless there are changes to the default configuration, this command fails:

```
--2009-05-06 23:00:54--  http://localhost/testfile
Resolving localhost... 127.0.0.1
Connecting to localhost|127.0.0.1|:80... connected.
HTTP request sent, awaiting response... 403 Forbidden
2009-05-06 23:00:54 ERROR 403: Forbidden.
```

8. As the Linux root user, run the `rm -i /var/www/html/testfile` command to remove `testfile`.

9. If you do not require `httpd` to be running, as the Linux root user, run the `service httpd stop` command to stop `httpd`:

```
# /sbin/service httpd stop
Stopping httpd:                                              [  OK  ]
```

This example demonstrates the additional security added by SELinux. Although DAC rules allowed the `httpd` process access to `testfile` in step 7, because the file was labeled with a type that the `httpd` process does not have access to, SELinux denied access. After step 7, an error similar to the following is logged to `/var/log/messages`:

```
May 6 23:00:54 localhost setroubleshoot: SELinux is preventing httpd (httpd_t)
"getattr"
to /var/www/html/testfile (samba_share_t). For complete SELinux messages.
run sealert -l c05911d3-e680-4e42-8e36-fe2ab9f8e654
```

Previous log files may use a `/var/log/messages.`*YYYYMMDD* format. When running **syslog-ng**, previous log files may use a `/var/log/messages.`*X* format. If the `setroubleshootd` and `auditd` processes are running, errors similar to the following are logged to `/var/log/audit/audit.log`:

```
type=AVC msg=audit(1220706212.937:70): avc:  denied  { getattr } for  pid=1904
comm="httpd" path="/var/www/html/testfile" dev=sda5 ino=247576
scontext=unconfined_u:system_r:httpd_t:s0
tcontext=unconfined_u:object_r:samba_share_t:s0  tclass=file

type=SYSCALL msg=audit(1220706212.937:70): arch=40000003 syscall=196 success=no
exit=-13 a0=b9e21da0 a1=bf9581dc a2=555ff4 a3=2008171 items=0 ppid=1902
```

```
pid=1904 auid=500 uid=48 gid=48 euid=48 suid=48 fsuid=48 egid=48 sgid=48
fsgid=48 tty=(none) ses=1 comm="httpd" exe="/usr/sbin/httpd"
subj=unconfined_u:system_r:httpd_t:s0 key=(null)
```

Also, an error similar to the following is logged to `/var/log/httpd/error_log`:

```
[Wed May 06 23:00:54 2009] [error] [client 127.0.0.1] (13)Permission denied:
access to /testfile denied
```

 **Note**

In Fedora 11, the setroubleshoot-server and audit packages are installed by default. These packages include the `setroubleshootd` and `auditd` daemons respectively. These daemons run by default. Stopping either of these daemons changes where SELinux denials are written to. Refer to *Section 5.2, "Which Log File is Used"* for further information.

4.2. Unconfined Processes

Unconfined processes run in unconfined domains, for example, init programs run in the unconfined `initrc_t` domain, unconfined kernel processes run in the `kernel_t` domain, and unconfined Linux users run in the `unconfined_t` domain. For unconfined processes, SELinux policy rules are applied, but policy rules exist that allow processes running in unconfined domains almost all access. Processes running in unconfined domains fall back to using DAC rules exclusively. If an unconfined process is compromised, SELinux does not prevent an attacker from gaining access to system resources and data, but of course, DAC rules are still used. SELinux is a security enhancement on top of DAC rules - it does not replace them.

The following example demonstrates how the Apache HTTP Server (`httpd`) can access data intended for use by Samba, when running unconfined. Note: in Fedora 11, the `httpd` process runs in the confined `httpd_t` domain by default. This is an example, and should not be used in production. It assumes that the httpd, wget, setroubleshoot-server, and audit packages are installed, that the SELinux targeted policy is used, and that SELinux is running in enforcing mode:

1. Run the `sestatus` command to confirm that SELinux is enabled, is running in enforcing mode, and that targeted policy is being used:

    ```
    $ /usr/sbin/sestatus
    SELinux status:                 enabled
    SELinuxfs mount:                /selinux
    Current mode:                   enforcing
    Mode from config file:          enforcing
    Policy version:                 23
    Policy from config file:        targeted
    ```

```
SELinux status: enabled
```
is returned when SELinux is enabled. `Current mode: enforcing` is returned when SELinux is running in enforcing mode. `Policy from config file: targeted` is returned when the SELinux targeted policy is used.

2. As the Linux root user, run the `touch /var/www/html/test2file` command to create a file.

3. Run the `ls -Z /var/www/html/test2file` command to view the SELinux context:

```
-rw-r--r--  root root unconfined_u:object_r:httpd_sys_content_t:s0
/var/www/html/test2file
```

By default, Linux users run unconfined in Fedora 11, which is why the `test2file` file is labeled with the SELinux `unconfined_u` user. RBAC is used for processes, not files. Roles do not have a meaning for files - the `object_r` role is a generic role used for files (on persistent storage and network file systems). Under the `/proc/` directory, files related to processes may use the `system_r` role.[3] The `httpd_sys_content_t` type allows the `httpd` process to access this file.

4. The `chcon` command relabels files; however, such label changes do not survive when the file system is relabeled. For permanent changes that survive a file system relabel, use the `semanage` command, which is discussed later. As the Linux root user, run the following command to change the type to a type used by Samba:

```
chcon -t samba_share_t /var/www/html/test2file
```

Run the `ls -Z /var/www/html/test2file` command to view the changes:

```
-rw-r--r--  root root unconfined_u:object_r:samba_share_t:s0
/var/www/html/test2file
```

5. Run the `service httpd status` command to confirm that the `httpd` process is not running:

```
$ /sbin/service httpd status
httpd is stopped
```

If the output differs, run the `service httpd stop` command as the Linux root user to stop the `httpd` process:

```
# /sbin/service httpd stop
Stopping httpd:                                            [  OK  ]
```

6. To make the `httpd` process run unconfined, run the following command as the Linux root user to change the type of `/usr/sbin/httpd`, to a type that does not transition to a confined domain:

```
chcon -t unconfined_exec_t /usr/sbin/httpd
```

---

[3] When using other policies, such as MLS, other roles may also be used, for example, `secadm_r`.

7. Run the `ls -Z /usr/sbin/httpd` command to confirm that `/usr/sbin/httpd` is labeled with the `unconfined_exec_t` type:

```
-rwxr-xr-x  root root system_u:object_r:unconfined_exec_t /usr/sbin/httpd
```

8. As the Linux root user, run the `service httpd start` command to start the `httpd` process. The output is as follows if `httpd` starts successfully:

```
# /sbin/service httpd start
Starting httpd:                                            [  OK  ]
```

9. Run the `ps -eZ | grep httpd` command to view the `httpd` running in the `unconfined_t` domain:

```
$ ps -eZ | grep httpd
unconfined_u:system_r:unconfined_t 7721 ?        00:00:00 httpd
unconfined_u:system_r:unconfined_t 7723 ?        00:00:00 httpd
unconfined_u:system_r:unconfined_t 7724 ?        00:00:00 httpd
unconfined_u:system_r:unconfined_t 7725 ?        00:00:00 httpd
unconfined_u:system_r:unconfined_t 7726 ?        00:00:00 httpd
unconfined_u:system_r:unconfined_t 7727 ?        00:00:00 httpd
unconfined_u:system_r:unconfined_t 7728 ?        00:00:00 httpd
unconfined_u:system_r:unconfined_t 7729 ?        00:00:00 httpd
unconfined_u:system_r:unconfined_t 7730 ?        00:00:00 httpd
```

10. Change into a directory where your Linux user has write access to, and run the `wget http://localhost/test2file` command. Unless there are changes to the default configuration, this command succeeds:

```
--2009-05-07 01:41:10--  http://localhost/test2file
Resolving localhost... 127.0.0.1
Connecting to localhost|127.0.0.1|:80... connected.
HTTP request sent, awaiting response... 200 OK
Length: 0 [text/plain]
Saving to: `test2file.1'

[ <=>                                   ]--.-K/s    in 0s

2009-05-07 01:41:10 (0.00 B/s) - `test2file.1' saved [0/0]
```

Although the `httpd` process does not have access to files labeled with the `samba_share_t` type, `httpd` is running in the unconfined `unconfined_t` domain, and falls back to using DAC rules, and as such, the `wget` command succeeds. Had `httpd` been running in the confined `httpd_t` domain, the `wget` command would have failed.

11. The `restorecon` command restores the default SELinux context for files. As the Linux root user, run the `restorecon -v /usr/sbin/httpd` command to restore the default SELinux context for `/usr/sbin/httpd`:

```
# /sbin/restorecon -v /usr/sbin/httpd
restorecon reset /usr/sbin/httpd context
system_u:object_r:unconfined_notrans_exec_t:s0-
>system_u:object_r:httpd_exec_t:s0
```

Run the `ls -Z /usr/sbin/httpd` command to confirm that `/usr/sbin/httpd` is labeled with the `httpd_exec_t` type:

```
$ ls -Z /usr/sbin/httpd
-rwxr-xr-x  root root system_u:object_r:httpd_exec_t    /usr/sbin/httpd
```

12. As the Linux root user, run the `/sbin/service httpd restart` command to restart `httpd`. After restarting, run the `ps -eZ | grep httpd` to confirm that `httpd` is running in the confined `httpd_t` domain:

```
# /sbin/service httpd restart
Stopping httpd:                                            [  OK  ]
Starting httpd:                                            [  OK  ]
# ps -eZ | grep httpd
unconfined_u:system_r:httpd_t     8880 ?        00:00:00 httpd
unconfined_u:system_r:httpd_t     8882 ?        00:00:00 httpd
unconfined_u:system_r:httpd_t     8883 ?        00:00:00 httpd
unconfined_u:system_r:httpd_t     8884 ?        00:00:00 httpd
unconfined_u:system_r:httpd_t     8885 ?        00:00:00 httpd
unconfined_u:system_r:httpd_t     8886 ?        00:00:00 httpd
unconfined_u:system_r:httpd_t     8887 ?        00:00:00 httpd
unconfined_u:system_r:httpd_t     8888 ?        00:00:00 httpd
unconfined_u:system_r:httpd_t     8889 ?        00:00:00 httpd
```

13. As the Linux root user, run the `rm -i /var/www/html/test2file` command to remove `test2file`.

14. If you do not require `httpd` to be running, as the Linux root user, run the `service httpd stop` command to stop `httpd`:

```
# /sbin/service httpd stop
Stopping httpd:                                            [  OK  ]
```

The examples in these sections demonstrate how data can be protected from a compromised confined-process (protected by SELinux), as well as how data is more accessible to an attacker from a compromised unconfined-process (not protected by SELinux).

4.3. Confined and Unconfined Users

Each Linux user is mapped to an SELinux user via SELinux policy. This allows Linux users to inherit the restrictions on SELinux users. This Linux user mapping is seen by running the `semanage login -l` command as the Linux root user:

```
# /usr/sbin/semanage login -l

Login Name                SELinux User            MLS/MCS Range
```

```
__default__                  unconfined_u              s0-s0:c0.c1023
root                         unconfined_u              s0-s0:c0.c1023
system_u                     system_u                  s0-s0:c0.c1023
```

In Fedora 11, Linux users are mapped to the SELinux `__default__` login by default (which is mapped to the SELinux `unconfined_u` user). The following defines the default-mapping:

```
__default__                  unconfined_u              s0-s0:c0.c1023
```

The following example demonstrates adding a new Linux user, and that Linux user being mapped to the SELinux `unconfined_u` user. It assumes that the Linux root user is running unconfined, as it does by default in Fedora 11:

1. As the Linux root user, run the `/usr/sbin/useradd newuser` command to create a new Linux user named newuser.

2. As the Linux root user, run the `passwd newuser` command to assign a password to the Linux newuser user:

    ```
    # passwd newuser
    Changing password for user newuser.
    New UNIX password: Enter a password
    Retype new UNIX password: Enter the same password again
    passwd: all authentication tokens updated successfully.
    ```

3. Log out of your current session, and log in as the Linux newuser user. When you log in, pam_selinux maps the Linux user to an SELinux user (in this case, unconfined_u), and sets up the resulting SELinux context. The Linux user's shell is then launched with this context. Run the `id -Z` command to view the context of a Linux user:

    ```
    [newuser@localhost ~]$ id -Z
    unconfined_u:unconfined_r:unconfined_t:s0-s0:c0.c1023
    ```

4. Log out of the Linux newuser's session, and log in with your account. If you do not want the Linux newuser user, run the `/usr/sbin/userdel -r newuser` command as the Linux root user to remove it, along with the Linux newuser's home directory.

Confined and unconfined Linux users are subject to executable and writeable memory checks, and are also restricted by MCS (and MLS, if the MLS policy is used). If unconfined Linux users execute an application that SELinux policy defines can transition from the `unconfined_t` domain to its own confined domain, unconfined Linux users are still subject to the restrictions of that confined domain. The security benefit of this is that, even though a Linux user is running unconfined, the application remains confined, and therefore, the exploitation of a flaw in the application can be limited by policy. Note: this does not protect the system from the user. Instead, the user and the system are being protected from possible damage caused by a flaw in the application.

The following confined SELinux users are available in Fedora 11:

User	Domain	X Window System	su and sudo	Execute in home directory and /tmp/	Networking
guest_u	guest_t	no	no	optional	no
xguest_u	xguest_t	yes	no	optional	only **Firefox**
user_u	user_t	yes	no	optional	yes
staff_u	staff_t	yes	only sudo	optional	yes

Table 4.1. SELinux User Capabilities

- Linux users in the `guest_t`, `xguest_t`, and `user_t` domains can only run set user ID (setuid) applications if SELinux policy permits it (such as `passwd`). They can not run the `su` and `/usr/bin/sudo` setuid applications, and therefore, can not use these applications to become the Linux root user.
- Linux users in the `guest_t` domain have no network access, and can only log in via a terminal (including `ssh`; they can log in via `ssh`, but can not use `ssh` to connect to another system).
- The only network access Linux users in the `xguest_t` domain have is **Firefox** connecting to web pages.
- Linux users in the `xguest_t`, `user_t` and `staff_t` domains can log in via the X Window System and a terminal.
- By default, Linux users in the `staff_t` domain do not have permissions to execute applications with `/usr/bin/sudo`. These permissions must be configured by an administrator.

By default, Linux users in the `guest_t` and `xguest_t` domains can not execute applications in their home directories or `/tmp/`, preventing them from executing applications (which inherit users' permissions) in directories they have write access to. This helps prevent flawed or malicious applications from modifying files users' own.

By default, Linux users in the `user_t` and `staff_t` domains can execute applications in their home directories and `/tmp/`. Refer to *Section 6.6, "Booleans for Users Executing Applications"* for information about allowing and preventing users from executing applications in their home directories and `/tmp/`.

Chapter 5.
Working with SELinux

The following sections give a brief overview of the main SELinux packages in Fedora 11; installing and updating packages; which log files are used; the main SELinux configuration file; enabling and disabling SELinux; SELinux modes; configuring Booleans; temporarily and persistently changing file and directory labels; overriding file system labels with the `mount` command; mounting NFS file systems; and how to preserve SELinux contexts when copying and archiving files and directories.

5.1. SELinux Packages

In Fedora 11, the SELinux packages are installed by default, unless they are manually excluded during installation. By default, SELinux targeted policy is used, and SELinux runs in enforcing mode. The following is a brief description of the main SELinux packages:

policycoreutils: provides utilities, such as `semanage`, `restorecon`, `audit2allow`, `semodule`, `load_policy`, and `setsebool`, for operating and managing SELinux.

policycoreutils-gui: provides `system-config-selinux`, a graphical tool for managing SELinux.

selinux-policy: provides the SELinux Reference Policy. The SELinux Reference Policy is a complete SELinux policy, and is used as a basis for other policies, such as the SELinux targeted policy. Refer to the Tresys Technology *SELinux Reference Policy*[1] page for further information. The selinux-policy-devel package provides development tools, such as `/usr/share/selinux/devel/policygentool` and `/usr/share/selinux/devel/policyhelp`, as well as example policy files. This package was merged into the selinux-policy package.

selinux-policy-`policy`: provides SELinux policies. For targeted policy, install selinux-policy-targeted. For MLS, install selinux-policy-mls. In Fedora 8, the strict policy was merged into targeted policy, allowing confined and unconfined users to co-exist on the same system.

setroubleshoot-server: translates denial messages, produced when access is denied by SELinux, into detailed descriptions that are viewed with `sealert` (which is provided by this package).

---

[1] *http://oss.tresys.com/projects/refpolicy*

setools, setools-gui, and setools-console: these packages provide the *Tresys Technology SETools distribution*[2], a number of tools and libraries for analyzing and querying policy, audit log monitoring and reporting, and file context management[3]. The setools package is a meta-package for SETools. The setools-gui package provides the `apol`, `seaudit`, and `sediffx` tools. The setools-console package provides the `seaudit-report`, `sechecker`, `sediff`, `seinfo`, `sesearch`, `findcon`, `replcon`, and `indexcon` command line tools. Refer to the *Tresys Technology SETools*[4] page for information about these tools.

libselinux-utils: provides the `avcstat`, `getenforce`, `getsebool`, `matchpathcon`, `selinuxconlist`, `selinuxdefcon`, `selinuxenabled`, `setenforce`, `togglesebool` tools.

mcstrans: translates levels, such as `s0-s0:c0.c1023`, to an easier to read form, such as `SystemLow-SystemHigh`. This package is not installed by default.

To install packages in Fedora 11, as the Linux root user, run the `yum install` *package-name* command. For example, to install the mcstrans package, run the `yum install mcstrans` command. To upgrade all installed packages in Fedora 11, run the `yum update` command.

Refer to *Managing Software with yum*[5-6] for further information about using `yum` to manage packages.

Note

In previous versions of Fedora, the selinux-policy-devel package is required when making a local policy module with `audit2allow -M`.

5.2. Which Log File is Used

In Fedora 11, the setroubleshoot-server and audit packages are installed if packages are not removed from the default package selection. These packages include the `setroubleshootd` and `auditd` daemons respectively. These daemons run by default.

SELinux denial messages, such as the following, are written to `/var/log/audit/audit.log` by default:

---

[2] *http://oss.tresys.com/projects/setools*

[3] Brindle, Joshua. "Re: blurb for fedora setools packages" Email to Murray McAllister. 1 November 2008. Any edits or changes in this version were done by Murray McAllister.

[4] *http://oss.tresys.com/projects/setools*

[5] Managing Software with yum, written by Stuart Ellis, edited by Paul W. Frields, Rodrigo Menezes, and Hugo Cisneiros.

[6] *http://docs.fedoraproject.org/yum/en/*

```
type=AVC msg=audit(1223024155.684:49): avc:   denied  { getattr } for  pid=2000
comm="httpd" path="/var/www/html/file1" dev=dm-0 ino=399185
scontext=unconfined_u:system_r:httpd_t:s0
tcontext=system_u:object_r:samba_share_t:s0 tclass=file
```

Also, if `setroubleshootd` is running, which it is by default, denial messages from `/var/log/audit/audit.log` are translated to an easier-to-read form and sent to `/var/log/messages`:

```
May  7 18:55:56 localhost setroubleshoot: SELinux is preventing httpd (httpd_t)
"getattr" to /var/www/html/file1 (samba_share_t). For complete SELinux
messages. run sealert -l de7e30d6-5488-466d-a606-92c9f40d316d
```

Denial messages are sent to a different location, depending on which daemons are running:

Daemon	*Log Location*
auditd on	`/var/log/audit/audit.log`
auditd off; rsyslogd on	`/var/log/messages`
setroubleshootd, rsyslogd, and auditd on	`/var/log/audit/audit.log`. Easier-to-read denial messages also sent to `/var/log/messages`

Starting Daemons Automatically

To configure the `auditd`, `rsyslogd`, and `setroubleshootd` daemons to automatically start at boot, run the following commands as the Linux root user:

```
/sbin/chkconfig --levels 2345 auditd on
```

```
/sbin/chkconfig --levels 2345 rsyslog on
```

```
/sbin/chkconfig --levels 345 setroubleshoot on
```

Use the `service service-name status` command to check if these services are running, for example:

```
$ /sbin/service auditd status
auditd (pid  1318) is running...
```

If the above services are not running (`service-name is stopped`), use the `service service-name start` command as the Linux root user to start them. For example:

```
# /sbin/service setroubleshoot start
Starting setroubleshootd:                                    [  OK  ]
```

5.3. Main Configuration File

The `/etc/selinux/config` file is the main SELinux configuration file. It controls the SELinux mode and the SELinux policy to use:

```
# This file controls the state of SELinux on the system.
# SELINUX= can take one of these three values:
#       enforcing - SELinux security policy is enforced.
#       permissive - SELinux prints warnings instead of enforcing.
#       disabled - No SELinux policy is loaded.
SELINUX=enforcing
# SELINUXTYPE= can take one of these two values:
#       targeted - Targeted processes are protected,
#       mls - Multi Level Security protection.
SELINUXTYPE=targeted
```

`SELINUX=enforcing`

The `SELINUX` option sets the mode SELinux runs in. SELinux has three modes: enforcing, permissive, and disabled. When using enforcing mode, SELinux policy is enforced, and SELinux denies access based on SELinux policy rules. Denial messages are logged. When using permissive mode, SELinux policy is not enforced. SELinux does not deny access, but denials are logged for actions that would have been denied if running SELinux in enforcing mode. When using disabled mode, SELinux is disabled (the SELinux module is not registered with the Linux kernel), and only DAC rules are used.

`SELINUXTYPE=targeted`

The `SELINUXTYPE` option sets the SELinux policy to use. Targeted policy is the default policy. Only change this option if you want to use the MLS policy. To use the MLS policy, install the selinux-policy-mls package; configure `SELINUXTYPE=mls` in `/etc/selinux/config`; and reboot your system.

 **Important**

When systems run with SELinux in permissive or disabled mode, users have permission to label files incorrectly. Also, files created while SELinux is disabled are not labeled. This causes problems when changing to enforcing mode. To prevent incorrectly labeled and unlabeled files from causing problems, file systems are automatically relabeled when changing from disabled mode to permissive or enforcing mode.

5.4. Enabling and Disabling SELinux

Use the `/usr/sbin/getenforce` or `/usr/sbin/sestatus` commands to check the status of SELinux. The `getenforce` command returns `Enforcing`, `Permissive`, or `Disabled`. The `getenforce` command returns `Enforcing` when SELinux is enabled (SELinux policy rules are enforced):

```
$ /usr/sbin/getenforce
Enforcing
```

The `getenforce` command returns `Permissive` when SELinux is enabled, but SELinux policy rules are not enforced, and only DAC rules are used. The `getenforce` command returns `Disabled` if SELinux is disabled.

The `sestatus` command returns the SELinux status and the SELinux policy being used:

```
$ /usr/sbin/sestatus
SELinux status:                 enabled
SELinuxfs mount:                /selinux
Current mode:                   enforcing
Mode from config file:          enforcing
Policy version:                 23
Policy from config file:        targeted
```

`SELinux status: enabled` is returned when SELinux is enabled. `Current mode: enforcing` is returned when SELinux is running in enforcing mode. `Policy from config file: targeted` is returned when the SELinux targeted policy is used.

5.4.1. Enabling SELinux

On systems with SELinux disabled, the `SELINUX=disabled` option is configured in `/etc/selinux/config`:

```
# This file controls the state of SELinux on the system.
# SELINUX= can take one of these three values:
#       enforcing - SELinux security policy is enforced.
#       permissive - SELinux prints warnings instead of enforcing.
#       disabled - No SELinux policy is loaded.
SELINUX=disabled
# SELINUXTYPE= can take one of these two values:
#       targeted - Targeted processes are protected,
#       mls - Multi Level Security protection.
SELINUXTYPE=targeted
```

Also, the `getenforce` command returns `Disabled`:

```
$ /usr/sbin/getenforce
Disabled
```

To enable SELinux:

1. Use the `rpm -qa | grep selinux`, `rpm -q policycoreutils`, and `rpm -qa | grep setroubleshoot` commands to confirm that the SELinux packages are installed. This guide assumes the following packages are installed: selinux-policy-targeted, selinux-policy, libselinux, libselinux-python, libselinux-utils, policycoreutils, setroubleshoot, setroubleshoot-server, setroubleshoot-plugins. If these packages are not installed, as the Linux root user, install them via the `yum install` *package-name* command. The following packages are optional: policycoreutils-gui, setroubleshoot, selinux-policy-devel, and mcstrans.

After installing the setroubleshoot-server package, use the `/sbin/chkconfig --list setroubleshoot` command to confirm that `setroubleshootd` starts when the system is running in runlevel[7] 3, 4, and 5:

```
$ /sbin/chkconfig --list setroubleshoot
setroubleshoot  0:off   1:off   2:off   3:on   4:on   5:on   6:off
```

If the output differs, as the Linux root user, run the `/sbin/chkconfig --levels 345 setroubleshoot on` command. This makes `setroubleshootd` automatically start when the system is in runlevel 3, 4, and 5.

2. Before SELinux is enabled, each file on the file system must be labeled with an SELinux context. Before this happens, confined domains may be denied access, preventing your system from booting correctly. To prevent this, configure `SELINUX=permissive` in `/etc/selinux/config`:

```
# This file controls the state of SELinux on the system.
# SELINUX= can take one of these three values:
#       enforcing - SELinux security policy is enforced.
#       permissive - SELinux prints warnings instead of enforcing.
#       disabled - No SELinux policy is loaded.
SELINUX=permissive
# SELINUXTYPE= can take one of these two values:
#       targeted - Targeted processes are protected,
#       mls - Multi Level Security protection.
SELINUXTYPE=targeted
```

3. As the Linux root user, run the `reboot` command to restart the system. During the next boot, file systems are labeled. The label process labels all files with an SELinux context:

```
*** Warning -- SELinux targeted policy relabel is required.
*** Relabeling could take a very long time, depending on file
*** system size and speed of hard drives.
****
```

Each * character on the bottom line represents 1000 files that have been labeled. In the above example, four * characters represent 4000 files have been labeled. The time it takes to label all files depends upon the number of files on the system, and the speed of the hard disk drives. On modern systems, this process can take as little as 10 minutes.

4. In permissive mode, SELinux policy is not enforced, but denials are still logged for actions that would have been denied if running in enforcing mode. Before changing to enforcing mode, as the Linux root user, run the `grep "SELinux is preventing" /var/log/messages` command as the Linux root user to confirm that SELinux did

---

[7] Refer to *http://en.wikipedia.org/wiki/Runlevel* for information about runlevels.

not deny actions during the last boot. If SELinux did not deny actions during the last boot, this command does not return any output. Refer to *Chapter 7, Troubleshooting for troubleshooting information if SELinux denied access during boot.*

5. If there were no denial messages in `/var/log/messages`, configure `SELINUX=enforcing` in `/etc/selinux/config`:

```
# This file controls the state of SELinux on the system.
# SELINUX= can take one of these three values:
#       enforcing - SELinux security policy is enforced.
#       permissive - SELinux prints warnings instead of enforcing.
#       disabled - No SELinux policy is loaded.
SELINUX=enforcing
# SELINUXTYPE= can take one of these two values:
#       targeted - Targeted processes are protected,
#       mls - Multi Level Security protection.
SELINUXTYPE=targeted
```

6. Reboot your system. After reboot, confirm that the `getenforce` command returns `Enforcing`:

```
$ /usr/sbin/getenforce
Enforcing
```

7. As the Linux root user, run the `/usr/sbin/semanage login -l` command to view the mapping between SELinux and Linux users. The output should be as follows:

```
Login Name              SELinux User            MLS/MCS Range

__default__             unconfined_u            s0-s0:c0.c1023
root                    unconfined_u            s0-s0:c0.c1023
system_u                system_u                s0-s0:c0.c1023
```

If this is not the case, run the following commands as the Linux root user to fix the user mappings. It is safe to ignore the `SELinux-user` *username* `is already defined` warnings if they occur, where *username* can be `unconfined_u`, `guest_u`, or `xguest_u`:

```
/usr/sbin/semanage user -a -S targeted -P user -R "unconfined_r system_r" -r
s0-s0:c0.c1023 unconfined_u
```

```
/usr/sbin/semanage login -m -S targeted -s "unconfined_u" -r s0-s0:c0.c1023
__default__
```

```
/usr/sbin/semanage login -m -S targeted -s "unconfined_u" -r s0-s0:c0.c1023
root
```

```
/usr/sbin/semanage user -a -S targeted -P user -R guest_r guest_u
```

```
/usr/sbin/semanage user -a -S targeted  -P user -R xguest_r xguest_u
```

Important

When systems run with SELinux in permissive or disabled mode, users have permission to label files incorrectly. Also, files created while SELinux is disabled are not labeled. This causes problems when changing to enforcing mode. To prevent incorrectly labeled and unlabeled files from causing problems, file systems are automatically relabeled when changing from disabled mode to permissive or enforcing mode.

5.4.2. Disabling SELinux

To disable SELinux, configure `SELINUX=disabled` in `/etc/selinux/config`:

```
# This file controls the state of SELinux on the system.
# SELINUX= can take one of these three values:
#       enforcing - SELinux security policy is enforced.
#       permissive - SELinux prints warnings instead of enforcing.
#       disabled - No SELinux policy is loaded.
SELINUX=disabled
# SELINUXTYPE= can take one of these two values:
#       targeted - Targeted processes are protected,
#       mls - Multi Level Security protection.
SELINUXTYPE=targeted
```

Reboot your system. After reboot, confirm that the `getenforce` command returns `Disabled`:

```
$ /usr/sbin/getenforce
Disabled
```

5.5. SELinux Modes

SELinux has three modes:

- Enforcing: SELinux policy is enforced. SELinux denies access based on SELinux policy rules.
- Permissive: SELinux policy is not enforced. SELinux does not deny access, but denials are logged for actions that would have been denied if running in enforcing mode.
- Disabled: SELinux is disabled. Only DAC rules are used.

Use the `/usr/sbin/setenforce` command to change between enforcing and permissive mode. Changes made with `/usr/sbin/setenforce` do not persist across reboots. To change to enforcing mode, as the Linux root user, run the `/usr/sbin/setenforce 1` command. To change to permissive mode, run the `/usr/sbin/setenforce 0` command. Use the `/usr/sbin/getenforce` command to view the current SELinux mode.

Persistent mode changes are covered in *Section 5.4, "Enabling and Disabling SELinux"*.

5.6. Booleans

Booleans allow parts of SELinux policy to be changed at runtime, without any knowledge of SELinux policy writing. This allows changes, such as allowing services access to NFS file systems, without reloading or recompiling SELinux policy.

5.6.1. Listing Booleans

For a list of Booleans, an explanation of what each one is, and whether they are on or off, run the `semanage boolean -l` command as the Linux root user. The following example does not list all Booleans:

```
# /usr/sbin/semanage boolean -l
SELinux boolean                         Description

ftp_home_dir                   -> off   Allow ftp to read and write files in
the user home directories
xen_use_nfs                    -> off   Allow xen to manage nfs files
xguest_connect_network         -> on    Allow xguest to configure Network
Manager
```

The `SELinux boolean` column lists Boolean names. The `Description` column lists whether the Booleans are on or off, and what they do.

In the following example, the `ftp_home_dir` Boolean is off, preventing the FTP daemon (`vsftpd`) from reading and writing to files in user home directories:

```
ftp_home_dir                   -> off   Allow ftp to read and write files in
the user home directories
```

The `getsebool -a` command lists Booleans, whether they are on or off, but does not give a description of each one. The following example does not list all Booleans:

```
$ /usr/sbin/getsebool -a
allow_console_login --> off
allow_cvs_read_shadow --> off
allow_daemons_dump_core --> on
```

Run the `getsebool` *boolean-name* command to only list the status of the *boolean-name* Boolean:

```
$ /usr/sbin/getsebool allow_console_login
allow_console_login --> off
```

Use a space-separated list to list multiple Booleans:

```
$ /usr/sbin/getsebool allow_console_login allow_cvs_read_shadow
allow_daemons_dump_core
allow_console_login --> off
allow_cvs_read_shadow --> off
allow_daemons_dump_core --> on
```

5.6.2. Configuring Booleans

The `setsebool` *boolean-name* *x* command turns Booleans on or off, where *boolean-name* is a Boolean name, and *x* is either `on` to turn the Boolean on, or `off` to turn it off.

The following example demonstrates configuring the `httpd_can_network_connect_db` Boolean:

1. By default, the `httpd_can_network_connect_db` Boolean is off, preventing Apache HTTP Server scripts and modules from connecting to database servers:

   ```
   $ /usr/sbin/getsebool httpd_can_network_connect_db
   httpd_can_network_connect_db --> off
   ```

2. To temporarily enable Apache HTTP Server scripts and modules to connect to database servers, run the `setsebool httpd_can_network_connect_db on` command as the Linux root user.

3. Use the `getsebool httpd_can_network_connect_db` command to verify the Boolean is turned on:

   ```
   $ /usr/sbin/getsebool httpd_can_network_connect_db
   httpd_can_network_connect_db --> on
   ```

   This allows Apache HTTP Server scripts and modules to connect to database servers.

4. This change is not persistent across reboots. To make changes persistent across reboots, run the `setsebool -P` *boolean-name* `on` command as the Linux root user:

   ```
   # /usr/sbin/setsebool -P httpd_can_network_connect_db on
   ```

5. To temporarily revert to the default behavior, as the Linux root user, run the `setsebool httpd_can_network_connect_db off` command. For changes that persist across reboots, run the `setsebool -P httpd_can_network_connect_db off` command.

5.6.3. Booleans for NFS and CIFS

By default, NFS mounts on the client side are labeled with a default context defined by policy for NFS file systems. In common policies, this default context uses the `nfs_t` type. Also, by default, Samba shares mounted on the client side are labeled with a default context defined by policy. In common policies, this default context uses the `cifs_t` type.

Depending on policy configuration, services may not be able to read files labeled with the `nfs_t` or `cifs_t` types. This may prevent file systems labeled with these types from being mounted and then read or exported by other services. Booleans can be turned on or off to control which services are allowed to access the `nfs_t` and `cifs_t` types.

The `setsebool` and `semanage` commands must be run as the Linux root user. The `setsebool -P` command makes persistent changes. Do not use the `-P` option if you do not want changes to persist across reboots:

Apache HTTP Server

To allow access to NFS file systems (files labeled with the `nfs_t` type):
```
/usr/sbin/setsebool -P httpd_use_nfs on
```
To allow access to Samba file systems (files labeled with the `cifs_t` type):
```
/usr/sbin/setsebool -P httpd_use_cifs on
```

Samba

To export NFS file systems:
```
/usr/sbin/setsebool -P samba_share_nfs on
```

FTP (`vsftpd`)

To allow access to NFS file systems:
```
/usr/sbin/setsebool -P allow_ftpd_use_nfs on
```
To allow access to Samba file systems:
```
/usr/sbin/setsebool -P allow_ftpd_use_cifs on
```

Other Services

For a list of NFS related Booleans for other services:
```
/usr/sbin/semanage boolean -l | grep nfs
```
For a list of Samba related Booleans for other services:
```
/usr/sbin/semanage boolean -l | grep cifs
```

 **Note**

These Booleans exist in SELinux policy as shipped with Fedora 11. They may not exist in policy shipped with other versions of Fedora or other operating systems.

5.7. SELinux Contexts - Labeling Files

On systems running SELinux, all processes and files are labeled with a label that contains security-relevant information. This information is called the SELinux context. For files, this is viewed using the `ls -Z` command:

```
$ ls -Z file1
-rw-rw-r--  user1 group1 unconfined_u:object_r:user_home_t:s0 file1
```

In this example, SELinux provides a user (`unconfined_u`), a role (`object_r`), a type (`user_home_t`), and a level (`s0`). This information is used to make access control decisions.

On DAC systems, access is controlled based on Linux user and group IDs. SELinux policy rules are checked after DAC rules. SELinux policy rules are not used if DAC rules deny access first.

There are multiple commands for managing the SELinux context for files, such as `chcon`, `semanage fcontext`, and `restorecon`.

5.7.1. Temporary Changes: chcon

The `chcon` command changes the SELinux context for files. These changes do not survive a file system relabel, or the `/sbin/restorecon` command. SELinux policy controls whether users are able to modify the SELinux context for any given file. When using `chcon`, users provide all or part of the SELinux context to change. An incorrect file type is a common cause of SELinux denying access.

Quick Reference

- Run the `chcon -t type file-name` command to change the file type, where `type` is a type, such as `httpd_sys_content_t`, and `file-name` is a file or directory name.
- Run the `chcon -R -t type directory-name` command to change the type of the directory and its contents, where `type` is a type, such as `httpd_sys_content_t`, and `directory-name` is a directory name.

Changing a File's or Directory's Type

The following example demonstrates changing the type, and no other attributes of the SELinux context:

1. Run the `cd` command without arguments to change into your home directory.

2. Run the `touch file1` command to create a new file. Use the `ls -Z file1` command to view the SELinux context for `file1`:

   ```
   $ ls -Z file1
   -rw-rw-r--  user1 group1 unconfined_u:object_r:user_home_t:s0 file1
   ```

   In this example, the SELinux context for `file1` includes the SELinux `unconfined_u` user, `object_r` role, `user_home_t` type, and the `s0` level. For a description of each part of the SELinux context, refer to *Chapter 3, SELinux Contexts*.

3. Run the `chcon -t samba_share_t file1` command to change the type to `samba_share_t`. The `-t` option only changes the type. View the change with `ls -Z file1`:

   ```
   $ ls -Z file1
   -rw-rw-r--  user1 group1 unconfined_u:object_r:samba_share_t:s0 file1
   ```

4. Use the `/sbin/restorecon -v file1` command to restore the SELinux context for the `file1` file. Use the `-v` option to view what changes:

```
$ /sbin/restorecon -v file1
restorecon reset file1 context unconfined_u:object_r:samba_share_t:s0-
>system_u:object_r:user_home_t:s0
```

   In this example, the previous type, `samba_share_t`, is restored to the correct, `user_home_t` type. When using targeted policy (the default SELinux policy in Fedora 11), the `/sbin/restorecon` command reads the files in the `/etc/selinux/targeted/contexts/files/` directory, to see which SELinux context files should have.

The example in this section works the same for directories, for example, if `file1` was a directory.

Changing a Directory and its Contents Types

The following example demonstrates creating a new directory, and changing the directory's file type (along with its contents) to a type used by the Apache HTTP Server. The configuration in this example is used if you want Apache HTTP Server to use a different document root (instead of `/var/www/html/`):

1. As the Linux root user, run the `mkdir /web` command to create a new directory, and then the `touch /web/file{1,2,3}` command to create 3 empty files (`file1`, `file2`, and `file3`). The `/web/` directory and files in it are labeled with the `default_t` type:

```
# ls -dZ /web
drwxr-xr-x  root root unconfined_u:object_r:default_t:s0 /web
# ls -lZ /web
-rw-r--r--  root root unconfined_u:object_r:default_t:s0 file1
-rw-r--r--  root root unconfined_u:object_r:default_t:s0 file2
-rw-r--r--  root root unconfined_u:object_r:default_t:s0 file3
```

2. As the Linux root user, run the `chcon -R -t httpd_sys_content_t /web/` command to change the type of the `/web/` directory (and its contents) to `httpd_sys_content_t`:

```
# chcon -R -t httpd_sys_content_t /web/
# ls -dZ /web/
drwxr-xr-x  root root unconfined_u:object_r:httpd_sys_content_t:s0 /web/
# ls -lZ /web/
-rw-r--r--  root root unconfined_u:object_r:httpd_sys_content_t:s0 file1
-rw-r--r--  root root unconfined_u:object_r:httpd_sys_content_t:s0 file2
-rw-r--r--  root root unconfined_u:object_r:httpd_sys_content_t:s0 file3
```

3. As the Linux root user, run the `/sbin/restorecon -R -v /web/` command to restore the default SELinux contexts:

```
# /sbin/restorecon -R -v /web/
restorecon reset /web context unconfined_u:object_r:httpd_sys_content_t:s0-
>system_u:object_r:default_t:s0
restorecon reset /web/file2 context
unconfined_u:object_r:httpd_sys_content_t:s0->system_u:object_r:default_t:s0
restorecon reset /web/file3 context
unconfined_u:object_r:httpd_sys_content_t:s0->system_u:object_r:default_t:s0
restorecon reset /web/file1 context
unconfined_u:object_r:httpd_sys_content_t:s0->system_u:object_r:default_t:s0
```

Refer to the chcon(1) manual page for further information about chcon.

 **Note**

> Type Enforcement is the main permission control used in SELinux targeted policy.
> For the most part, SELinux users and roles can be ignored.

5.7.2. Persistent Changes: semanage fcontext

The /usr/sbin/semanage fcontext command changes the SELinux context for files.
When using targeted policy, changes made with this command are added to the
/etc/selinux/targeted/contexts/files/file_contexts file if the changes are to files
that exists in file_contexts, or are added to file_contexts.local for new files and
directories, such as creating a /web/ directory. setfiles, which is used when a file system
is relabeled, and /sbin/restorecon, which restores the default SELinux contexts, read
these files. This means that changes made by /usr/sbin/semanage fcontext are
persistent, even if the file system is relabeled. SELinux policy controls whether users are
able to modify the SELinux context for any given file.

Quick Reference

To make SELinux context changes that survive a file system relabel:

1. Run the /usr/sbin/semanage fcontext -a *options file-name|directory-name*
    command, remembering to use the full path to the file or directory.

2. Run the /sbin/restorecon -v *file-name|directory-name* command to apply the
    context changes.

Changing a File's Type

The following example demonstrates changing a file's type, and no other attributes of the
SELinux context:

1. As the Linux root user, run the touch /etc/file1 command to create a new file. By
    default, newly-created files in the /etc/ directory are labeled with the etc_t type:
    ```
    # ls -Z /etc/file1
    -rw-r--r--  root root unconfined_u:object_r:etc_t:s0        /etc/file1
    ```

2. As the Linux root user, run the `/usr/sbin/semanage fcontext -a -t samba_share_t /etc/file1` command to change the `file1` type to `samba_share_t`. The `-a` option adds a new record, and the `-t` option defines a type (`samba_share_t`). Note: running this command does not directly change the type - `file1` is still labeled with the `etc_t` type:

```
# /usr/sbin/semanage fcontext -a -t samba_share_t /etc/file1
# ls -Z /etc/file1
-rw-r--r--   root root unconfined_u:object_r:etc_t:s0        /etc/file1
```

The `/usr/sbin/semanage fcontext -a -t samba_share_t /etc/file1` command adds the following entry to `/etc/selinux/targeted/contexts/files/file_contexts.local`:

```
/etc/file1     unconfined_u:object_r:samba_share_t:s0
```

3. As the Linux root user, run the `/sbin/restorecon -v /etc/file1` command to change the type. Since the `semanage` command added an entry to `file.contexts.local` for `/etc/file1`, the `/sbin/restorecon` command changes the type to `samba_share_t`:

```
# /sbin/restorecon -v /etc/file1
restorecon reset /etc/file1 context unconfined_u:object_r:etc_t:s0-
>system_u:object_r:samba_share_t:s0
```

4. As the Linux root user, run the `rm -i /etc/file1` command to remove `file1`.

5. As the Linux root user, run the `/usr/sbin/semanage fcontext -d /etc/file1` command to remove the context added for `/etc/file1`. When the context is removed, running `restorecon` changes the type to `etc_t`, rather than `samba_share_t`.

Changing a Directory's Type

The following example demonstrates creating a new directory and changing that directory's file type, to a type used by Apache HTTP Server:

1. As the Linux root user, run the `mkdir /web` command to create a new directory. This directory is labeled with the `default_t` type:

```
# ls -dZ /web
drwxr-xr-x   root root unconfined_u:object_r:default_t:s0 /web
```

The `ls -d` option makes `ls` list information about a directory, rather than its contents, and the `-Z` option makes `ls` display the SELinux context (in this example, `unconfined_u:object_r:default_t:s0`).

2. As the Linux root user, run the `/usr/sbin/semanage fcontext -a -t httpd_sys_content_t /web` command to change the `/web/` type to `httpd_sys_content_t`. The `-a` option adds a new record, and the `-t` option defines

a type (`httpd_sys_content_t`). Note: running this command does not directly change the type - /web/ is still labeled with the `default_t` type:

```
# /usr/sbin/semanage fcontext -a -t httpd_sys_content_t /web
# ls -dZ /web
drwxr-xr-x  root root unconfined_u:object_r:default_t:s0    /web
```

The `/usr/sbin/semanage fcontext -a -t httpd_sys_content_t /web` command adds the following entry to `/etc/selinux/targeted/contexts/files/file_contexts.local`:

```
/web    unconfined_u:object_r:httpd_sys_content_t:s0
```

3. As the Linux root user, run the `/sbin/restorecon -v /web` command to change the type. Since the `semanage` command added an entry to `file.contexts.local` for /web, the `/sbin/restorecon` command changes the type to `httpd_sys_content_t`:

```
# /sbin/restorecon -v /web
restorecon reset /web context unconfined_u:object_r:default_t:s0-
>system_u:object_r:httpd_sys_content_t:s0
```

By default, newly-created files and directories inherit the SELinux type of their parent folders. When using this example, and before removing the SELinux context added for /web/, files and directories created in the /web/ directory are labeled with the `httpd_sys_content_t` type.

4. As the Linux root user, run the `/usr/sbin/semanage fcontext -d /web` command to remove the context added for /web/.

5. As the Linux root user, run the `/sbin/restorecon -v /web` command to restore the default SELinux context.

Changing a Directory and its Contents Types

The following example demonstrates creating a new directory, and changing the directory's file type (along with its contents) to a type used by Apache HTTP Server. The configuration in this example is used if you want Apache HTTP Server to use a different document root (instead of /var/www/html/):

1. As the Linux root user, run the `mkdir /web` command to create a new directory, and then the `touch /web/file{1,2,3}` command to create 3 empty files (`file1`, `file2`, and `file3`). The /web/ directory and files in it are labeled with the `default_t` type:

```
# ls -dZ /web
drwxr-xr-x  root root unconfined_u:object_r:default_t:s0 /web
# ls -lZ /web
-rw-r--r--  root root unconfined_u:object_r:default_t:s0 file1
-rw-r--r--  root root unconfined_u:object_r:default_t:s0 file2
-rw-r--r--  root root unconfined_u:object_r:default_t:s0 file3
```

2. As the Linux root user, run the `/usr/sbin/semanage fcontext -a -t httpd_sys_content_t "/web(/.*)?"` command to change the type of the `/web/` directory and the files in it, to `httpd_sys_content_t`. The `-a` option adds a new record, and the `-t` option defines a type (httpd_sys_content_t). The `"/web(/.*)?"` regular expression causes the `semanage` command to apply changes to the `/web/` directory, as well as the files in it. Note: running this command does not directly change the type - `/web/` and files in it are still labeled with the `default_t` type:

```
# ls -dZ /web
drwxr-xr-x  root root unconfined_u:object_r:default_t:s0 /web
# ls -lZ /web
-rw-r--r--  root root unconfined_u:object_r:default_t:s0 file1
-rw-r--r--  root root unconfined_u:object_r:default_t:s0 file2
-rw-r--r--  root root unconfined_u:object_r:default_t:s0 file3
```

The `/usr/sbin/semanage fcontext -a -t httpd_sys_content_t "/web(/.*)?"` command adds the following entry to `/etc/selinux/targeted/contexts/files/file_contexts.local`:

```
/web(/.*)?     system_u:object_r:httpd_sys_content_t:s0
```

3. As the Linux root user, run the `/sbin/restorecon -R -v /web` command to change the type of the `/web/` directory, as well as all files in it. The `-R` is for recursive, which means all files and directories under the `/web/` directory are labeled with the `httpd_sys_content_t` type. Since the `semanage` command added an entry to `file.contexts.local` for `/web(/.*)?`, the `/sbin/restorecon` command changes the types to `httpd_sys_content_t`:

```
# /sbin/restorecon -R -v /web
restorecon reset /web context unconfined_u:object_r:default_t:s0-
>system_u:object_r:httpd_sys_content_t:s0
restorecon reset /web/file2 context unconfined_u:object_r:default_t:s0-
>system_u:object_r:httpd_sys_content_t:s0
restorecon reset /web/file3 context unconfined_u:object_r:default_t:s0-
>system_u:object_r:httpd_sys_content_t:s0
restorecon reset /web/file1 context unconfined_u:object_r:default_t:s0-
>system_u:object_r:httpd_sys_content_t:s0
```

By default, newly-created files and directories inherit the SELinux type of their parents. In this example, files and directories created in the `/web/` directory will be labeled with the `httpd_sys_content_t` type.

4. As the Linux root user, run the `/usr/sbin/semanage fcontext -d "/web(/.*)?"` command to remove the context added for `"/web(/.*)?"`.

5. As the Linux root user, run the `/sbin/restorecon -R -v /web` command to restore the default SELinux contexts.

Deleting an added Context

The following example demonstrates adding and removing an SELinux context:

1. As the Linux root user, run the `/usr/sbin/semanage fcontext -a -t httpd_sys_content_t /test` command. The `/test/` directory does not have to exist. This command adds the following context to `/etc/selinux/targeted/contexts/files/file_contexts.local`:

   ```
   /test     system_u:object_r:httpd_sys_content_t:s0
   ```

2. To remove the context, as the Linux root user, run the `/usr/sbin/semanage fcontext -d` *file-name*|*directory-name* command, where *file-name*|*directory-name* is the first part in `file_contexts.local`. The following is an example of a context in `file_contexts.local`:

   ```
   /test     system_u:object_r:httpd_sys_content_t:s0
   ```

   With the first part being `/test`. To prevent the `/test/` directory from being labeled with the `httpd_sys_content_t` after running `/sbin/restorecon`, or after a file system relabel, run the following command as the Linux root user to delete the context from `file_contexts.local`:

   ```
   /usr/sbin/semanage fcontext -d /test
   ```

If the context is part of a regular expression, for example, `/web(/.*)?`, use quotation marks around the regular expression:

```
/usr/sbin/semanage fcontext -d "/web(/.*)?"
```

Refer to the semanage(8) manual page for further information about `/usr/sbin/semanage`.

Important

When changing the SELinux context with `/usr/sbin/semanage fcontext -a`, use the full path to the file or directory to avoid files being mislabeled after a file system relabel, or after the `/sbin/restorecon` command is run.

5.8. The file_t and default_t Types

On file systems that support extended attributes, when a file that lacks an SELinux context on disk is accessed, it is treated as if it had a default context as defined by SELinux policy. In common policies, this default context uses the `file_t` type. This should be the only use of this type, so that files without a context on disk can be distinguished in policy, and generally kept inaccessible to confined domains. The `file_t` type should not exist on correctly-labeled file systems, because all files on a system running SELinux should have an SELinux context, and the `file_t` type is never used in file-context configuration[8].

The `default_t` type is used on files that do not match any other pattern in file-context configuration, so that such files can be distinguished from files that do not have a context on disk, and generally kept inaccessible to confined domains. If you create a new top-level directory, such as `/mydirectory/`, this directory may be labeled with the `default_t` type. If services need access to such a directory, update the file-contexts configuration for this location. Refer to *Section 5.7.2, "Persistent Changes: semanage fcontext"* for details on adding a context to the file-context configuration.

5.9. Mounting File Systems

By default, when a file system that supports extended attributes is mounted, the security context for each file is obtained from the *security.selinux* extended attribute of the file. Files in file systems that do not support extended attributes are assigned a single, default security context from the policy configuration, based on file system type.

Use the `mount -o context` command to override existing extended attributes, or to specify a different, default context for file systems that do not support extended attributes. This is useful if you do not trust a file system to supply the correct attributes, for example, removable media used in multiple systems. The `mount -o context` command can also be used to support labeling for file systems that do not support extended attributes, such as File Allocation Table (FAT) or NFS file systems. The context specified with the `context` is not written to disk: the original contexts are preserved, and are seen when mounting without a `context` option (if the file system had extended attributes in the first place).

For further information about file system labeling, refer to James Morris's "Filesystem Labeling in SELinux" article: *http://www.linuxjournal.com/article/7426*.

5.9.1. Context Mounts

To mount a file system with the specified context, overriding existing contexts if they exist, or to specify a different, default context for a file system that does not support extended attributes, as the Linux root user, use the `mount -o context=SELinux_user:role:type:level` command when mounting the desired file system. Context changes are not written to disk. By default, NFS mounts on the client side are labeled with a default context defined by policy for NFS file systems. In common

---

[8] Files in `/etc/selinux/targeted/contexts/files/` define contexts for files and directories. Files in this directory are read by `restorecon` and `setfiles` to restore files and directories to their default contexts.

policies, this default context uses the `nfs_t` type. Without additional mount options, this may prevent sharing NFS file systems via other services, such as the Apache HTTP Server. The following example mounts an NFS file system so that it can be shared via the Apache HTTP Server:

```
# mount server:/export /local/mount/point -o\
context="system_u:object_r:httpd_sys_content_t:s0"
```

Newly-created files and directories on this file system appear to have the SELinux context specified with `-o context`; however, since context changes are not written to disk for these situations, the context specified with the `context` option is only retained if the `context` option is used on the next mount, and if the same context is specified.

Type Enforcement is the main permission control used in SELinux targeted policy. For the most part, SELinux users and roles can be ignored, so, when overriding the SELinux context with `-o context`, use the SELinux `system_u` user and `object_r` role, and concentrate on the type. If you are not using the MLS policy or multi-category security, use the `s0` level.

Note

When a file system is mounted with a `context` option, context changes (by users and processes) are prohibited. For example, running `chcon` on a file system mounted with a `context` option results in a `Operation not supported` error.

5.9.2. Changing the Default Context

As mentioned in *Section 5.8, "The file_t and default_t Types"*, on file systems that support extended attributes, when a file that lacks an SELinux context on disk is accessed, it is treated as if it had a default context as defined by SELinux policy. In common policies, this default context uses the `file_t` type. If it is desirable to use a different default context, mount the file system with the `defcontext` option.

The following example mounts a newly-created file system (on `/dev/sda2`) to the newly-created `/test/` directory. It assumes that there are no rules in `/etc/selinux/targeted/contexts/files/` that define a context for the `/test/` directory:

```
# mount /dev/sda2 /test/ -o defcontext="system_u:object_r:samba_share_t:s0"
```

In this example:

- the `defcontext` option defines that `system_u:object_r:samba_share_t:s0` is "the default security context for unlabeled files"[9].

---

[9] Morris, James. "Filesystem Labeling in SELinux". Published 1 October 2004. Accessed 14 October 2008: *http://www.linuxjournal.com/article/7426*.

- when mounted, the root directory (`/test/`) of the file system is treated as if it is labeled with the context specified by `defcontext` (this label is not stored on disk). This affects the labeling for files created under `/test/`: new files inherit the `samba_share_t` type, and these labels are stored on disk.

- files created under `/test/` while the file system was mounted with a `defcontext` option retain their labels.

5.9.3. Mounting an NFS File System

By default, NFS mounts on the client side are labeled with a default context defined by policy for NFS file systems. In common policies, this default context uses the `nfs_t` type. Depending on policy configuration, services, such as Apache HTTP Server and MySQL, may not be able to read files labeled with the `nfs_t` type. This may prevent file systems labeled with this type from being mounted and then read or exported by other services.

If you would like to mount an NFS file system and read or export that file system with another service, use the `context` option when mounting to override the `nfs_t` type. Use the following context option to mount NFS file systems so that they can be shared via the Apache HTTP Server:

```
mount server:/export /local/mount/point -o\
context="system_u:object_r:httpd_sys_content_t:s0"
```

Since context changes are not written to disk for these situations, the context specified with the `context` option is only retained if the `context` option is used on the next mount, and if the same context is specified.

As an alternative to mounting file systems with `context` options, Booleans can be turned on to allow services access to file systems labeled with the `nfs_t` type. Refer to *Section 5.6.3, "Booleans for NFS and CIFS"* for instructions on configuring Booleans to allow services access to the `nfs_t` type.

5.9.4. Multiple NFS Mounts

When mounting multiple mounts from the same NFS export, attempting to override the SELinux context of each mount with a different context, results in subsequent mount commands failing. In the following example, the NFS server has a single export, `/export`, which has two subdirectories, `web/` and `database/`. The following commands attempt two mounts from a single NFS export, and try to override the context for each one:

```
# mount server:/export/web /local/web -o\
context="system_u:object_r:httpd_sys_content_t:s0"

# mount server:/export/database /local/database -o\
context="system_u:object_r:mysqld_db_t:s0"
```

The second mount command fails, and the following is logged to `/var/log/messages`:

```
kernel: SELinux: mount invalid.  Same superblock, different security settings
for (dev 0:15, type nfs)
```

To mount multiple mounts from a single NFS export, with each mount having a different context, use the `-o nosharecache,context` options. The following example mounts multiple mounts from a single NFS export, with a different context for each mount (allowing a single service access to each one):

```
# mount server:/export/web /local/web -o\
nosharecache,context="system_u:object_r:httpd_sys_content_t:s0"

# mount server:/export/database /local/database -o\
nosharecache,context="system_u:object_r:mysqld_db_t:s0"
```

In this example, `server:/export/web` is mounted locally to `/local/web/`, with all files being labeled with the `httpd_sys_content_t` type, allowing Apache HTTP Server access. `server:/export/database` is mounted locally to `/local/database`, with all files being labeled with the `mysqld_db_t` type, allowing MySQL access. These type changes are not written to disk.

 **Important**

> The `nosharecache` options allows you to mount the same subdirectory of an export multiple times with different contexts (for example, mounting `/export/web` multiple times). Do not mount the same subdirectory from an export multiple times with different contexts, as this creates an overlapping mount, where files are accessible under two different contexts.

5.9.5. Making Context Mounts Persistent

To make context mounts persistent across remounting and reboots, add entries for the file systems in `/etc/fstab` or an automounter map, and use the desired context as a mount option. The following example adds an entry to `/etc/fstab` for an NFS context mount:

```
server:/export /local/mount/ nfs
context="system_u:object_r:httpd_sys_content_t:s0" 0 0
```

Refer to the *Red Hat Enterprise Linux 5 Deployment Guide, Section 19.2. "NFS Client Configuration"*[10] for information about mounting NFS file systems.

---

[10] http://www.redhat.com/docs/en-US/Red_Hat_Enterprise_Linux/5.2/html/Deployment_Guide/s1-nfs-client-config.html

5.10. Maintaining SELinux Labels

These sections describe what happens to SELinux contexts when copying, moving, and archiving files and directories. Also, it explains how to preserve contexts when copying and archiving.

5.10.1. Copying Files and Directories

When a file or directory is copied, a new file or directory is created if it does not exist. That new file or directory's context is based on default-labeling rules, not the original file or directory's context (unless options were used to preserve the original context). For example, files created in user home directories are labeled with the user_home_t type:

```
$ touch file1
$ ls -Z file1
-rw-rw-r--  user1 group1 unconfined_u:object_r:user_home_t:s0 file1
```

If such a file is copied to another directory, such as /etc/, the new file is created in accordance to default-labeling rules for the /etc/ directory. Copying a file (without additional options) may not preserve the original context:

```
$ ls -Z file1
-rw-rw-r--  user1 group1 unconfined_u:object_r:user_home_t:s0 file1
# cp file1 /etc/
$ ls -Z /etc/file1
-rw-r--r--  root root unconfined_u:object_r:etc_t:s0    /etc/file1
```

When file1 is copied to /etc/, if /etc/file1 does not exist, /etc/file1 is created as a new file. As shown in the example above, /etc/file1 is labeled with the etc_t type, in accordance to default-labeling rules.

When a file is copied over an existing file, the existing file's context is preserved, unless the user specified cp options to preserve the context of the original file, such as --preserve=context. SELinux policy may prevent contexts from being preserved during copies.

Copying Without Preserving SELinux Contexts

When copying a file with the cp command, if no options are given, the type is inherited from the targeted, parent directory:

```
$ touch file1
$ ls -Z file1
-rw-rw-r--  user1 group1 unconfined_u:object_r:user_home_t:s0 file1
$ ls -dZ /var/www/html/
drwxr-xr-x  root root system_u:object_r:httpd_sys_content_t:s0 /var/www/html/
# cp file1 /var/www/html/
$ ls -Z /var/www/html/file1
```

```
-rw-r--r--  root root unconfined_u:object_r:httpd_sys_content_t:s0
/var/www/html/file1
```

In this example, `file1` is created in a user's home directory, and is labeled with the
`user_home_t` type. The `/var/www/html/` directory is labeled with the
`httpd_sys_content_t` type, as shown with the `ls -dZ /var/www/html/` command. When
`file1` is copied to `/var/www/html/`, it inherits the `httpd_sys_content_t` type, as shown
with the `ls -Z /var/www/html/file1` command.

Preserving SELinux Contexts When Copying

Use the `cp --preserve=context` command to preserve contexts when copying:

```
$ touch file1
$ ls -Z file1
-rw-rw-r--  user1 group1 unconfined_u:object_r:user_home_t:s0 file1
$ ls -dZ /var/www/html/
drwxr-xr-x  root root system_u:object_r:httpd_sys_content_t:s0 /var/www/html/
# cp --preserve=context file1 /var/www/html/
$ ls -Z /var/www/html/file1
-rw-r--r--  root root unconfined_u:object_r:user_home_t:s0 /var/www/html/file1
```

In this example, `file1` is created in a user's home directory, and is labeled with the
`user_home_t` type. The `/var/www/html/` directory is labeled with the
`httpd_sys_content_t` type, as shown with the `ls -dZ /var/www/html/` command. Using
the `--preserve=context` option preserves SELinux contexts during copy operations. As
shown with the `ls -Z /var/www/html/file1` command, the `file1 user_home_t` type was
preserved when the file was copied to `/var/www/html/`.

Copying and Changing the Context

Use the `cp -Z` command to change the destination copy's context. The following example
was performed in the user's home directory:

```
$ touch file1
$ cp -Z system_u:object_r:samba_share_t:s0 file1 file2
$ ls -Z file1 file2
-rw-rw-r--  user1 group1 unconfined_u:object_r:user_home_t:s0 file1
-rw-rw-r--  user1 group1 system_u:object_r:samba_share_t:s0 file2
$ rm file1 file2
```

In this example, the context is defined with the `-Z` option. Without the `-Z` option, `file2`
would be labeled with the `unconfined_u:object_r:user_home_t` context.

Copying a File Over an Existing File

When a file is copied over an existing file, the existing file's context is preserved (unless an
option is used to preserve contexts). For example:

```
# touch /etc/file1
# ls -Z /etc/file1
-rw-r--r--   root root unconfined_u:object_r:etc_t:s0     /etc/file1
# touch /tmp/file2
# ls -Z /tmp/file2
-rw-r--r--   root root unconfined_u:object_r:user_tmp_t:s0 /tmp/file2
# cp /tmp/file2 /etc/file1
# ls -Z /etc/file1
-rw-r--r--   root root unconfined_u:object_r:etc_t:s0     /etc/file1
```

In this example, two files are created: /etc/file1, labeled with the etc_t type, and /tmp/file2, labeled with the user_tmp_t type. The cp /tmp/file2 /etc/file1 command overwrites file1 with file2. After copying, the ls -Z /etc/file1 command shows file1 labeled with the etc_t type, not the user_tmp_t type from /tmp/file2 that replaced /etc/file1.

Important

Copy files and directories, rather than moving them. This helps ensure they are labeled with the correct SELinux contexts. Incorrect SELinux contexts can prevent processes from accessing such files and directories.

5.10.2. Moving Files and Directories

File and directories keep their current SELinux context when they are moved. In many cases, this is incorrect for the location they are being moved to. The following example demonstrates moving a file from a user's home directory to /var/www/html/, which is used by the Apache HTTP Server. Since the file is moved, it does not inherit the correct SELinux context:

1. Run the cd command without any arguments to change into your home directory. Once in your home directory, run the touch file1 command to create a file. This file is labeled with the user_home_t type:

    ```
    $ ls -Z file1
    -rw-rw-r--   user1 group1 unconfined_u:object_r:user_home_t:s0 file1
    ```

2. Run the ls -dZ /var/www/html/ command to view the SELinux context of the /var/www/html/ directory:

    ```
    $ ls -dZ /var/www/html/
    drwxr-xr-x   root root system_u:object_r:httpd_sys_content_t:s0
    /var/www/html/
    ```

    By default, the /var/www/html/ directory is labeled with the httpd_sys_content_t type. Files and directories created under the /var/www/html/ directory inherit this type, and as such, they are labeled with this type.

3. As the Linux root user, run the `mv file1 /var/www/html/` command to move `file1` to the `/var/www/html/` directory. Since this file is moved, it keeps its current `user_home_t` type:

```
# mv file1 /var/www/html/
# ls -Z /var/www/html/file1
-rw-rw-r--  user1 group1 unconfined_u:object_r:user_home_t:s0
/var/www/html/file1
```

By default, the Apache HTTP Server can not read files that are labeled with the `user_home_t` type. If all files comprising a web page are labeled with the `user_home_t` type, or another type that the Apache HTTP Server can not read, permission is denied when attempting to access them via Firefox or text-based Web browsers.

 **Important**

> Moving files and directories with the `mv` command may result in the wrong SELinux context, preventing processes, such as the Apache HTTP Server and Samba, from accessing such files and directories.

5.10.3. Checking the Default SELinux Context

Use the `/usr/sbin/matchpathcon` command to check if files and directories have the correct SELinux context. From the matchpathcon(8) manual page: "`matchpathcon` queries the system policy and outputs the default security context associated with the file path."[11]. The following example demonstrates using the `/usr/sbin/matchpathcon` command to verify that files in `/var/www/html/` directory are labeled correctly:

1. As the Linux root user, run the `touch /var/www/html/file{1,2,3}` command to create three files (`file1`, `file2`, and `file3`). These files inherit the `httpd_sys_content_t` type from the `/var/www/html/` directory:

```
# touch /var/www/html/file{1,2,3}
# ls -Z /var/www/html/
-rw-r--r--  root root unconfined_u:object_r:httpd_sys_content_t:s0 file1
-rw-r--r--  root root unconfined_u:object_r:httpd_sys_content_t:s0 file2
-rw-r--r--  root root unconfined_u:object_r:httpd_sys_content_t:s0 file3
```

2. As the Linux root user, run the `chcon -t samba_share_t /var/www/html/file1` command to change the `file1` type to `samba_share_t`. Note: the Apache HTTP Server can not read files or directories labeled with the `samba_share_t` type.

---

[11] The matchpathcon(8) manual page, as shipped with the libselinux-utils package in Fedora, is written by Daniel Walsh. Any edits or changes in this version were done by Murray McAllister.

3. The `/usr/sbin/matchpathcon -V` option compares the current SELinux context to the correct, default context in SELinux policy. Run the `/usr/sbin/matchpathcon -V /var/www/html/*` command to check all files in the `/var/www/html/` directory:

```
$ /usr/sbin/matchpathcon -V /var/www/html/*
/var/www/html/file1 has context unconfined_u:object_r:samba_share_t:s0,
should be system_u:object_r:httpd_sys_content_t:s0
/var/www/html/file2 verified.
/var/www/html/file3 verified.
```

The following output from the `/usr/sbin/matchpathcon` command explains that `file1` is labeled with the `samba_share_t` type, but should be labeled with the `httpd_sys_content_t` type:

```
/var/www/html/file1 has context unconfined_u:object_r:samba_share_t:s0, should
be system_u:object_r:httpd_sys_content_t:s0
```

To resolve the label problem and allow the Apache HTTP Server access to `file1`, as the Linux root user, run the `/sbin/restorecon -v /var/www/html/file1` command:

```
# /sbin/restorecon -v /var/www/html/file1
restorecon reset /var/www/html/file1 context
unconfined_u:object_r:samba_share_t:s0-
>system_u:object_r:httpd_sys_content_t:s0
```

5.10.4. Archiving Files with tar

`tar` does not retain extended attributes by default. Since SELinux contexts are stored in extended attributes, contexts can be lost when archiving files. Use `tar --selinux` to create archives that retain contexts. If a Tar archive contains files without extended attributes, or if you want the extended attributes to match the system defaults, run the archive through `/sbin/restorecon`:

```
$ tar -xvf archive.tar | /sbin/restorecon -f -
```

Note: depending on the directory, you may need to be the Linux root user to run the `/sbin/restorecon` command.

The following example demonstrates creating a Tar archive that retains SELinux contexts:

1. As the Linux root user, run the `touch /var/www/html/file{1,2,3}` command to create three files (`file1`, `file2`, and `file3`). These files inherit the `httpd_sys_content_t` type from the `/var/www/html/` directory:

```
# touch /var/www/html/file{1,2,3}
# ls -Z /var/www/html/
-rw-r--r--  root root unconfined_u:object_r:httpd_sys_content_t:s0 file1
-rw-r--r--  root root unconfined_u:object_r:httpd_sys_content_t:s0 file2
-rw-r--r--  root root unconfined_u:object_r:httpd_sys_content_t:s0 file3
```

2. Run the `cd /var/www/html/` command to change into the `/var/www/html/` directory. Once in this directory, as the Linux root user, run the `tar --selinux -cf test.tar file{1,2,3}` command to create a Tar archive named `test.tar`.

3. As the Linux root user, run the `mkdir /test` command to create a new directory, and then, run the `chmod 777 /test/` command to allow all users full-access to the `/test/` directory.

4. Run the `cp /var/www/html/test.tar /test/` command to copy the `test.tar` file in to the `/test/` directory.

5. Run the `cd /test/` command to change into the `/test/` directory. Once in this directory, run the `tar -xvf test.tar` command to extract the Tar archive.

6. Run the `ls -lZ /test/` command to view the SELinux contexts. The `httpd_sys_content_t` type has been retained, rather than being changed to `default_t`, which would have happened had the `--selinux` not been used:

```
$ ls -lZ /test/
-rw-r--r--  user1 group1 unconfined_u:object_r:httpd_sys_content_t:s0 file1
-rw-r--r--  user1 group1 unconfined_u:object_r:httpd_sys_content_t:s0 file2
-rw-r--r--  user1 group1 unconfined_u:object_r:httpd_sys_content_t:s0 file3
-rw-r--r--  user1 group1 unconfined_u:object_r:default_t:s0 test.tar
```

7. If the `/test/` directory is no longer required, as the Linux root user, run the `rm -ri /test/` command to remove it, as well as all files in it.

Refer to the tar(1) manual page for further information about `tar`, such as the `--xattrs` option that retains all extended attributes.

5.10.5. Archiving Files with star

`star` does not retain extended attributes by default. Since SELinux contexts are stored in extended attributes, contexts can be lost when archiving files. Use `star -xattr -H=exustar` to create archives that retain contexts. The star package is not installed by default. To install `star`, run the `yum install star` command as the Linux root user.

The following example demonstrates creating a Star archive that retains SELinux contexts:

1. As the Linux root user, run the `touch /var/www/html/file{1,2,3}` command to create three files (`file1`, `file2`, and `file3`). These files inherit the `httpd_sys_content_t` type from the `/var/www/html/` directory:

```
# touch /var/www/html/file{1,2,3}
# ls -Z /var/www/html/
-rw-r--r--  root root unconfined_u:object_r:httpd_sys_content_t:s0 file1
-rw-r--r--  root root unconfined_u:object_r:httpd_sys_content_t:s0 file2
-rw-r--r--  root root unconfined_u:object_r:httpd_sys_content_t:s0 file3
```

2. Run the `cd /var/www/html/` command to change into the `/var/www/html/` directory. Once in this directory, as the Linux root user, run the `star -xattr -H=exustar -c -f=test.star file{1,2,3}` command to create a Star archive named `test.star`:

```
# star -xattr -H=exustar -c -f=test.star file{1,2,3}
star: 1 blocks + 0 bytes (total of 10240 bytes = 10.00k).
```

3. As the Linux root user, run the `mkdir /test` command to create a new directory, and then, run the `chmod 777 /test/` command to allow all users full-access to the `/test/` directory.

4. Run the `cp /var/www/html/test.star /test/` command to copy the `test.star` file in to the `/test/` directory.

5. Run the `cd /test/` command to change into the `/test/` directory. Once in this directory, run the `star -x -f=test.star` command to extract the Star archive:

```
$ star -x -f=test.star
star: 1 blocks + 0 bytes (total of 10240 bytes = 10.00k).
```

6. Run the `ls -lZ /test/` command to view the SELinux contexts. The `httpd_sys_content_t` type has been retained, rather than being changed to `default_t`, which would have happened had the `--selinux` not been used:

```
$ ls -lZ /test/
-rw-r--r--   user1 group1 unconfined_u:object_r:httpd_sys_content_t:s0 file1
-rw-r--r--   user1 group1 unconfined_u:object_r:httpd_sys_content_t:s0 file2
-rw-r--r--   user1 group1 unconfined_u:object_r:httpd_sys_content_t:s0 file3
-rw-r--r--   user1 group1 unconfined_u:object_r:default_t:s0 test.star
```

7. If the `/test/` directory is no longer required, as the Linux root user, run the `rm -ri /test/` command to remove it, as well as all files in it.

8. If `star` is no longer required, as the Linux root user, run the `yum remove star` command to remove the package.

Refer to the star(1) manual page for further information about `star`.

Chapter 6.
Confining Users

A number of confined SELinux users are available in Fedora 11. Each Linux user is mapped to an SELinux user via SELinux policy, allowing Linux users to inherit the restrictions on SELinux users, for example (depending on the user), not being able to: run the X Window System; use networking; run setuid applications (unless SELinux policy permits it); or run the `su` and `sudo` commands to become the Linux root user. This helps protect the system from the user. Refer to *Section 4.3, "Confined and Unconfined Users"* for further information about confined users in Fedora 11.

6.1. Linux and SELinux User Mappings

As the Linux root user, run the `semanage login -l` command to view the mapping between Linux users and SELinux users:

```
# /usr/sbin/semanage login -l

Login Name                      SELinux User                MLS/MCS Range

__default__                     unconfined_u                s0-s0:c0.c1023
root                            unconfined_u                s0-s0:c0.c1023
system_u                        system_u                    s0-s0:c0.c1023
```

In Fedora 11, Linux users are mapped to the SELinux `__default__` login by default (which is mapped to the SELinux `unconfined_u` user). When a Linux user is created with the `useradd` command, if no options are specified, they are mapped to the SELinux `unconfined_u` user. The following defines the default-mapping:

```
__default__                     unconfined_u                s0-s0:c0.c1023
```

6.2. Confining New Linux Users: useradd

Linux users mapped to the SELinux `unconfined_u` user run in the `unconfined_t` domain. This is seen by running the `id -Z` command while logged-in as a Linux user mapped to `unconfined_u`:

```
$ id -Z
unconfined_u:unconfined_r:unconfined_t:s0-s0:c0.c1023
```

When Linux users run in the `unconfined_t` domain, SELinux policy rules are applied, but policy rules exist that allow Linux users running in the `unconfined_t` domain almost all access. If unconfined Linux users execute an application that SELinux policy defines can transition from the `unconfined_t` domain to its own confined domain, unconfined Linux users are still subject to the restrictions of that confined domain. The security benefit of this is that, even though a Linux user is running unconfined, the application remains confined, and therefore, the exploitation of a flaw in the application can be limited by policy. Note: this does not protect the system from the user. Instead, the user and the system are being protected from possible damage caused by a flaw in the application.

When creating Linux users with `useradd`, use the `-Z` option to specify which SELinux user they are mapped to. The following example creates a new Linux user, useruuser, and maps that user to the SELinux `user_u` user. Linux users mapped to the SELinux `user_u` user run in the `user_t` domain. In this domain, Linux users are unable to run setuid applications unless SELinux policy permits it (such as `passwd`), and can not run `su` or `sudo`, preventing them from becoming the Linux root user with these commands.

1. As the Linux root user, run the `/usr/sbin/useradd -Z user_u useruuser` command to create a new Linux user (useruuser) that is mapped to the SELinux `user_u` user.

2. As the Linux root user, run the `semanage login -l` command to view the mapping between the Linux `useruuser` user and `user_u`:

```
# /usr/sbin/semanage login -l

Login Name              SELinux User            MLS/MCS Range

__default__             unconfined_u            s0-s0:c0.c1023
root                    unconfined_u            s0-s0:c0.c1023
system_u                system_u                s0-s0:c0.c1023
useruuser               user_u                  s0
```

3. As the Linux root user, run the `passwd useruuser` command to assign a password to the Linux useruuser user:

```
# passwd useruuser
Changing password for user useruuser.
New UNIX password: Enter a password
Retype new UNIX password: Enter the same password again
passwd: all authentication tokens updated successfully.
```

4. Log out of your current session, and log in as the Linux useruuser user. When you log in, pam_selinux maps the Linux user to an SELinux user (in this case, `user_u`), and sets up the resulting SELinux context. The Linux user's shell is then launched with this context. Run the `id -Z` command to view the context of a Linux user:

```
[useruuser@localhost ~]$ id -Z
user_u:user_r:user_t:s0
```

5. Log out of the Linux useruuser's session, and log back in with your account. If you do not want the Linux useruuser user, run the `/usr/sbin/userdel -r useruuser` command as the Linux root user to remove it, along with its home directory.

6.3. Confining Existing Linux Users: semanage login

If a Linux user is mapped to the SELinux `unconfined_u` user (the default behavior), and you would like to change which SELinux user they are mapped to, use the `semanage login` command. The following example creates a new Linux user named newuser, then maps that Linux user to the SELinux `user_u` user:

1. As the Linux root user, run the `/usr/sbin/useradd newuser` command to create a new Linux user (newuser). Since this user uses the default mapping, it does not appear in the `/usr/sbin/semanage login -l` output:

```
# /usr/sbin/semanage login -l

Login Name              SELinux User            MLS/MCS Range
__default__             unconfined_u            s0-s0:c0.c1023
root                    unconfined_u            s0-s0:c0.c1023
system_u                system_u                s0-s0:c0.c1023
```

2. To map the Linux newuser user to the SELinux `user_u` user, run the following command as the Linux root user:

```
/usr/sbin/semanage login -a -s user_u newuser
```

The `-a` option adds a new record, and the `-s` option specifies the SELinux user to map a Linux user to. The last argument, `newuser`, is the Linux user you want mapped to the specified SELinux user.

3. To view the mapping between the Linux newuser user and `user_u`, run the `semanage login -l` command as the Linux root user:

```
# /usr/sbin/semanage login -l

Login Name              SELinux User            MLS/MCS Range
__default__             unconfined_u            s0-s0:c0.c1023
newuser                 user_u                  s0
root                    unconfined_u            s0-s0:c0.c1023
system_u                system_u                s0-s0:c0.c1023
```

4. As the Linux root user, run the `passwd newuser` command to assign a password to the Linux newuser user:

```
# passwd newuser
Changing password for user newuser.
New UNIX password: Enter a password
Retype new UNIX password: Enter the same password again
passwd: all authentication tokens updated successfully.
```

5. Log out of your current session, and log in as the Linux newuser user. Run the `id -Z` command to view the newuser's SELinux context:

```
[newuser@rlocalhost ~]$ id -Z
user_u:user_r:user_t:s0
```

6. Log out of the Linux newuser's session, and log back in with your account. If you do not want the Linux newuser user, run the `userdel -r newuser` command as the Linux root user to remove it, along with its home directory. Also, the mapping between the Linux newuser user and `user_u` is removed:

```
# /usr/sbin/userdel -r newuser
# /usr/sbin/semanage login -l

Login Name                SELinux User              MLS/MCS Range

__default__               unconfined_u              s0-s0:c0.c1023
root                      unconfined_u              s0-s0:c0.c1023
system_u                  system_u                  s0-s0:c0.c1023
```

6.4. Changing the Default Mapping

In Fedora 11, Linux users are mapped to the SELinux `__default__` login by default (which is mapped to the SELinux `unconfined_u` user). If you would like new Linux users, and Linux users not specifically mapped to an SELinux user to be confined by default, change the default mapping with the `semanage login` command.

For example, run the following command as the Linux root user to change the default mapping from `unconfined_u` to `user_u`:

`/usr/sbin/semanage login -m -S targeted -s "user_u" -r s0 __default__`

Run the `semanage login -l` command as the Linux root user to verify the `__default__` login is mapped to `user_u`:

```
# /usr/sbin/semanage login -l

Login Name                SELinux User              MLS/MCS Range

__default__               user_u                    s0
root                      unconfined_u              s0-s0:c0.c1023
system_u                  system_u                  s0-s0:c0.c1023
```

If a new Linux user is created and an SELinux user is not specified, or if an existing Linux user logs in and does not match a specific entry from the `semanage login -l` output, they are mapped to `user_u`, as per the `__default__` login.

To change back to the default behavior, run the following command as the Linux root user to map the `__default__` login to the SELinux `unconfined_u` user:

```
/usr/sbin/semanage login -m -S targeted -s "unconfined_u" -r\
s0-s0:c0.c1023 __default__
```

6.5. xguest: Kiosk Mode

The xguest package provides a kiosk user account. This account is used to secure machines that people walk up to and use, such as those at libraries, banks, airports, information kiosks, and coffee shops. The kiosk user account is very locked down: essentially, it only allows users to log in and use **Firefox** to browse Internet websites. Any changes made while logged in with his account, such as creating files or changing settings, are lost when you log out.

To set up the kiosk account:

1. As the Linux root user, run `yum install xguest` command to install the xguest package. Install dependencies as required.

2. In order to allow the kiosk account to be used by a variety of people, the account is not password-protected, and as such, the account can only be protected if SELinux is running in enforcing mode. Before logging in with this account, use the `getenforce` command to confirm that SELinux is running in enforcing mode:

   ```
   $ /usr/sbin/getenforce
   Enforcing
   ```

   If this is not the case, refer to *Section 5.5, "SELinux Modes"* for information about changing to enforcing mode. It is not possible to log in with this account if SELinux is in permissive mode or disabled.

3. You can only log in to this account via the GNOME Display Manager (GDM). Once the xguest package is installed, a `Guest` account is added to GDM. To log in, click on the `Guest` account:

6.6. Booleans for Users Executing Applications

Not allowing Linux users to execute applications (which inherit users' permissions) in their home directories and /tmp/, which they have write access to, helps prevent flawed or malicious applications from modifying files users' own. In Fedora 11, by default, Linux users in the guest_t and xguest_t domains can not execute applications in their home directories or /tmp/; however, by default, Linux users in the user_t and staff_t domains can.

Booleans are available to change this behavior, and are configured with the setsebool command. The setsebool command must be run as the Linux root user. The setsebool -P command makes persistent changes. Do not use the -P option if you do not want changes to persist across reboots:

guest_t

To *allow* Linux users in the guest_t domain to execute applications in their home directories and /tmp/:

```
/usr/sbin/setsebool -P allow_guest_exec_content on
```

xguest_t

To *allow* Linux users in the xguest_t domain to execute applications in their home directories and /tmp/:

```
/usr/sbin/setsebool -P allow_xguest_exec_content on
```

user_t

To *prevent* Linux users in the user_t domain from executing applications in their home directories and /tmp/:

```
/usr/sbin/setsebool -P allow_user_exec_content off
```

staff_t

To *prevent* Linux users in the staff_t domain from executing applications in their home directories and /tmp/:

```
/usr/sbin/setsebool -P allow_staff_exec_content off
```

Chapter 7. Troubleshooting

The following chapter describes what happens when SELinux denies access; the top three causes of problems; where to find information about correct labeling; analyzing SELinux denials; and creating custom policy modules with `audit2allow`.

7.1. What Happens when Access is Denied

SELinux decisions, such as allowing or disallowing access, are cached. This cache is known as the Access Vector Cache (AVC). Denial messages are logged when SELinux denies access. These denials are also known as "AVC denials", and are logged to a different location, depending on which daemons are running:

Daemon	Log Location
auditd on	`/var/log/audit/audit.log`
auditd off; rsyslogd on	`/var/log/messages`
setroubleshootd, rsyslogd, and auditd on	`/var/log/audit/audit.log`. Easier-to-read denial messages also sent to `/var/log/messages`

If you are running the X Window System, have the setroubleshoot and setroubleshoot-server packages installed, and the `setroubleshootd` and `auditd` daemons are running, a yellow star and a warning are displayed when access is denied by SELinux:

Clicking on the star presents a detailed analysis of why SELinux denied access, and a possible solution for allowing access. If you are not running the X Window System, it is less obvious when access is denied by SELinux. For example, users browsing your website may receive an error similar to the following:

```
Forbidden

You don't have permission to access file name on this server
```

For these situations, if DAC rules (standard Linux permissions) allow access, check /var/log/messages and /var/log/audit/audit.log for "SELinux is preventing" and "denied" errors respectively. This can be done by running the following commands as the Linux root user:

```
grep "SELinux is preventing" /var/log/messages
grep "denied" /var/log/audit/audit.log
```

7.2. Top Three Causes of Problems

The following sections describe the top three causes of problems: labeling problems, configuring Booleans and ports for services, and evolving SELinux rules.

7.2.1. Labeling Problems

On systems running SELinux, all processes and files are labeled with a label that contains security-relevant information. This information is called the SELinux context. If these labels are wrong, access may be denied. If an application is labeled incorrectly, the process it transitions to may not have the correct label, possibly causing SELinux to deny access, and the process being able to create mislabeled files.

A common cause of labeling problems is when a non-standard directory is used for a service. For example, instead of using /var/www/html/ for a website, an administrator wants to use /srv/myweb/. On Fedora 11, the /srv/ directory is labeled with the var_t type. Files and directories created and /srv/ inherit this type. Also, newly-created top-level directories (such as /myserver/) may be labeled with the default_t type. SELinux prevents the Apache HTTP Server (httpd) from accessing both of these types. To allow access, SELinux must know that the files in /srv/myweb/ are to be accessible to httpd:

```
# /usr/sbin/semanage fcontext -a -t httpd_sys_content_t \
"/srv/myweb(/.*)?"
```

This semanage command adds the context for the /srv/myweb/ directory (and all files and directories under it) to the SELinux file-context configuration[1]. The semanage command

---

[1] Files in /etc/selinux/targeted/contexts/files/ define contexts for files and directories. Files in this directory are read by restorecon and setfiles to restore files and directories to their default contexts.

does not change the context. As the Linux root user, run the `restorecon` command to apply the changes:

```
# /sbin/restorecon -R -v /srv/myweb
```

Refer to *Section 5.7.2, "Persistent Changes: semanage fcontext"* for further information about adding contexts to the file-context configuration.

7.2.1.1. What is the Correct Context?

The `matchpathcon` command checks the context of a file path and compares it to the default label for that path. The following example demonstrates using `matchpathcon` on a directory that contains incorrectly labeled files:

```
$ /usr/sbin/matchpathcon -V /var/www/html/*
/var/www/html/index.html has context unconfined_u:object_r:user_home_t:s0,
should be system_u:object_r:httpd_sys_content_t:s0
/var/www/html/page1.html has context unconfined_u:object_r:user_home_t:s0,
should be system_u:object_r:httpd_sys_content_t:s0
```

In this example, the `index.html` and `page1.html` files are labeled with the `user_home_t` type. This type is used for files in user home directories. Using the `mv` command to move files from your home directory may result in files being labeled with the `user_home_t` type. This type should not exist outside of home directories. Use the `restorecon` command to restore such files to their correct type:

```
# /sbin/restorecon -v /var/www/html/index.html
restorecon reset /var/www/html/index.html context
unconfined_u:object_r:user_home_t:s0->system_u:object_r:httpd_sys_content_t:s0
```

To restore the context for all files under a directory, use the `-R` option:

```
# /sbin/restorecon -R -v /var/www/html/
restorecon reset /var/www/html/page1.html context
unconfined_u:object_r:samba_share_t:s0-
>system_u:object_r:httpd_sys_content_t:s0
restorecon reset /var/www/html/index.html context
unconfined_u:object_r:samba_share_t:s0-
>system_u:object_r:httpd_sys_content_t:s0
```

Refer to *Section 5.10.3, "Checking the Default SELinux Context"* for a more detailed example of `matchpathcon`.

7.2.2. How are Confined Services Running?

Services can be run in a variety of ways. To cater for this, you must tell SELinux how you are running services. This can be achieved via Booleans that allow parts of SELinux policy to be changed at runtime, without any knowledge of SELinux policy writing. This allows changes, such as allowing services access to NFS file systems, without reloading or recompiling SELinux policy. Also, running services on non-default port numbers requires policy configuration to be updated via the `semanage` command.

For example, to allow the Apache HTTP Server to communicate with MySQL, turn the `httpd_can_network_connect_db` Boolean on:

```
# /usr/sbin/setsebool -P httpd_can_network_connect_db on
```

If access is denied for a particular service, use the `getsebool` and `grep` commands to see if any Booleans are available to allow access. For example, use the `getsebool -a | grep ftp` command to search for FTP related Booleans:

```
$ /usr/sbin/getsebool -a | grep ftp
allow_ftpd_anon_write --> off
allow_ftpd_full_access --> off
allow_ftpd_use_cifs --> off
allow_ftpd_use_nfs --> off
ftp_home_dir --> off
httpd_enable_ftp_server --> off
tftp_anon_write --> off
```

For a list of Booleans and whether they are on or off, run the `/usr/sbin/getsebool -a` command. For a list of Booleans, an explanation of what each one is, and whether they are on or off, run the `/usr/sbin/semanage boolean -l` command as the Linux root user. Refer to *Section 5.6, "Booleans"* for information about listing and configuring Booleans.

Port Numbers

Depending on policy configuration, services may only be allowed to run on certain port numbers. Attempting to change the port a service runs on without changing policy may result in the service failing to start. For example, run the `semanage port -l | grep http` command as the Linux root user to list `http` related ports:

```
# /usr/sbin/semanage port -l | grep http
http_cache_port_t              tcp      3128, 8080, 8118
http_cache_port_t              udp      3130
http_port_t                    tcp      80, 443, 488, 8008, 8009, 8443
pegasus_http_port_t            tcp      5988
pegasus_https_port_t           tcp      5989
```

The `http_port_t` port type defines the ports Apache HTTP Server can listen on, which in this case, are TCP ports 80, 443, 488, 8008, 8009, and 8443. If an administrator configures `httpd.conf` so that `httpd` listens on port 9876 (`Listen 9876`), but policy is not updated to reflect this, the `service httpd start` command fails:

```
# /sbin/service httpd start
Starting httpd: (13)Permission denied: make_sock: could not bind to address
[::]:9876
(13)Permission denied: make_sock: could not bind to address 0.0.0.0:9876
no listening sockets available, shutting down
```

```
Unable to open logs
                                                          [FAILED]
```

An SELinux denial similar to the following is logged to `/var/log/audit/audit.log`:

```
type=AVC msg=audit(1225948455.061:294): avc:  denied  { name_bind } for
pid=4997 comm="httpd" src=9876 scontext=unconfined_u:system_r:httpd_t:s0
tcontext=system_u:object_r:port_t:s0 tclass=tcp_socket
```

To allow `httpd` to listen on a port that is not listed for the `http_port_t` port type, run the `semanage port` command to add a port to policy configuration[2]:

```
# /usr/sbin/semanage port -a -t http_port_t -p tcp 9876
```

The `-a` option adds a new record; the `-t` option defines a type; and the `-p` option defines a protocol. The last argument is the port number to add.

7.2.3. Evolving Rules and Broken Applications

Applications may be broken, causing SELinux to deny access. Also, SELinux rules are evolving - SELinux may not have seen an application running in a certain way, possibly causing it to deny access, even though the application is working as expected. For example, if a new version of PostgreSQL is released, it may perform actions the current policy has not seen before, causing access to be denied, even though access should be allowed.

For these situations, after access is denied, use `audit2allow` to create a custom policy module to allow access. Refer to *Section 7.3.8, "Allowing Access: audit2allow"* for information about using `audit2allow`.

7.3. Fixing Problems

The following sections help troubleshoot issues. They go over: checking Linux permissions, which are checked before SELinux rules; possible causes of SELinux denying access, but no denials being logged; manual pages for services, which contain information about labeling and Booleans; permissive domains, for allowing one process to run permissive, rather than the whole system; how to search for and view denial messages; analyzing denials; and creating custom policy modules with `audit2allow`.

7.3.1. Linux Permissions

When access is denied, check standard Linux permissions. As mentioned in *Chapter 2, Introduction*, most operating systems use a Discretionary Access Control (DAC) system to

---

[2] The `semanage port -a` command adds an entry to the `/etc/selinux/targeted/modules/active/ports.local` file. Note: by default, this file can only be viewed by the Linux root user.

control access, allowing users to control the permissions of files that they own. SELinux policy rules are checked after DAC rules. SELinux policy rules are not used if DAC rules deny access first.

If access is denied and no SELinux denials are logged, use the `ls -l` command to view the standard Linux permissions:

```
$ ls -l /var/www/html/index.html
-rw-r----- 1 root root 0 2009-05-07 11:06 index.html
```

In this example, `index.html` is owned by the root user and group. The root user has read and write permissions (`-rw`), and members of the root group have read permissions (`-r-`). Everyone else has no access (`---`). By default, such permissions do not allow `httpd` to read this file. To resolve this issue, use the `chown` command to change the owner and group. This command must be run as the Linux root user:

```
# chown apache:apache /var/www/html/index.html
```

This assumes the default configuration, in which `httpd` runs as the Linux apache user. If you run `httpd` with a different user, replace `apache:apache` with that user.

Refer to the *Fedora Documentation Project "Permissions"*[3] draft for information about managing Linux permissions.

7.3.2. Possible Causes of Silent Denials

In certain situations, AVC denials may not be logged when SELinux denies access. Applications and system library functions often probe for more access than required to perform their tasks. To maintain least privilege without filling audit logs with AVC denials for harmless application probing, the policy can silence AVC denials without allowing a permission by using `dontaudit` rules. These rules are common in standard policy. The downside of `dontaudit` is that, although SELinux denies access, denial messages are not logged, making troubleshooting hard.

To temporarily disable `dontaudit` rules, allowing all denials to be logged, run the following command as the Linux root user:

```
/usr/sbin/semodule -DB
```

The `-D` option disables `dontaudit` rules; the `-B` option rebuilds policy. After running `semodule -DB`, try exercising the application that was encountering permission problems, and see if SELinux denials — relevant to the application — are now being logged. Take care in deciding which denials should be allowed, as some should be ignored and handled via

---

[3] *http://fedoraproject.org/wiki/Docs/Drafts/AdministrationGuide/Permissions*

`dontaudit` rules. If in doubt, or in search of guidance, contact other SELinux users and developers on an SELinux list, such as *fedora-selinux-list*[4].

To rebuild policy and enable `dontaudit` rules, run the following command as the Linux root user:

```
/usr/sbin/semodule -B
```

This restores the policy to its original state. For a full list of `dontaudit` rules, run the `sesearch --dontaudit` command. Narrow down searches using the `-s domain` option and the `grep` command. For example:

```
$ sesearch --dontaudit -s smbd_t | grep squid
WARNING: This policy contained disabled aliases; they have been removed.
dontaudit smbd_t squid_port_t : tcp_socket name_bind ;
dontaudit smbd_t squid_port_t : udp_socket name_bind ;
```

Refer to *Section 7.3.6, "Raw Audit Messages"* and *Section 7.3.7, "sealert Messages"* for information about analyzing denials.

7.3.3. Manual Pages for Services

Manual pages for services contain valuable information, such as what file type to use for a given situation, and Booleans to change the access a service has (such as `httpd` accessing NFS file systems). This information may be in the standard manual page, or a manual page with `selinux` prepended or appended.

For example, the httpd_selinux(8) manual page has information about what file type to use for a given situation, as well as Booleans to allow scripts, sharing files, accessing directories inside user home directories, and so on. Other manual pages with SELinux information for services include:

- Samba: the samba_selinux(8) manual page describes that files and directories to be exported via Samba must be labeled with the `samba_share_t` type, as well as Booleans to allow files labeled with types other than `samba_share_t` to be exported via Samba.
- NFS: the nfs_selinux(8) manual page describes that, by default, file systems can not be exported via NFS, and that to allow file systems to be exported, Booleans such as `nfs_export_all_ro` or `nfs_export_all_rw` must be turned on.
- Berkeley Internet Name Domain (BIND): the named(8) manual page describes what file type to use for a given situation (see the `Red Hat SELinux BIND Security Profile` section). The named_selinux(8) manual page describes that, by default, `named` can not write to master zone files, and to allow such access, the `named_write_master_zones` Boolean must be turned on.

---

[4] *http://www.redhat.com/mailman/listinfo/fedora-selinux-list*

The information in manual pages helps you configure the correct file types and Booleans, helping to prevent SELinux from denying access.

7.3.4. Permissive Domains

When SELinux is running in permissive mode, SELinux does not deny access, but denials are logged for actions that would have been denied if running in enforcing mode. Previously, it was not possible to make a single domain permissive (remember: processes run in domains). In certain situations, this led to making the whole system permissive to troubleshoot issues.

Fedora 11 introduces permissive domains, where an administrator can configure a single process (domain) to run permissive, rather than making the whole system permissive. SELinux checks are still performed for permissive domains; however, the kernel allows access and reports an AVC denial for situations where SELinux would have denied access. Permissive domains are also available in Fedora 9 (with the latest updates applied).

In Red Hat Enterprise Linux 4 and 5, `domain_disable_trans` Booleans are available to prevent an application from transitioning to a confined domain, and therefore, the process runs in an unconfined domain, such as `initrc_t`. Turning such Booleans on can cause major problems. For example, if the `httpd_disable_trans` Boolean is turned on:

- `httpd` runs in the unconfined `initrc_t` domain. Files created by processes running in the `initrc_t` domain may not have the same labeling rules applied as files created by a process running in the `httpd_t` domain, potentially allowing processes to create mislabeled files. This causes access problems later on.
- confined domains that are allowed to communicate with `httpd_t` can not communicate with `initrc_t`, possibly causing additional failures.

The `domain_disable_trans` Booleans were removed from Fedora 7, even though there was no replacement. Permissive domains solve the above issues: transition rules apply, and files are created with the correct labels.

Permissive domains can be used for:

- making a single process (domain) run permissive to troubleshoot an issue, rather than putting the entire system at risk by making the entire system permissive.
- creating policies for new applications. Previously, it was recommended that a minimal policy be created, and then the entire machine put into permissive mode, so that the application could run, but SELinux denials still logged. `audit2allow` could then be used to help write the policy. This put the whole system at risk. With permissive domains, only the domain in the new policy can be marked permissive, without putting the whole system at risk.

7.3.4.1. Making a Domain Permissive

To make a domain permissive, run the `semanage permissive -a` *domain* command, where *domain* is the domain you want to make permissive. For example, run the following command as the Linux root user to make the `httpd_t` domain (the domain the Apache HTTP Server runs in) permissive:

```
/usr/sbin/semanage permissive -a httpd_t
```

To view a list of domains you have made permissive, run the `semodule -l | grep permissive` command as the Linux root user. For example:

```
# /usr/sbin/semodule -l | grep permissive
permissive_httpd_t        1.0
```

If you no longer want a domain to be permissive, run the `semanage permissive -d` *domain* command as the Linux root user. For example:

```
/usr/sbin/semanage permissive -d httpd_t
```

7.3.4.2. Denials for Permissive Domains

The `SYSCALL` message is different for permissive domains. The following is an example AVC denial (and the associated system call) from the Apache HTTP Server:

```
type=AVC msg=audit(1226882736.442:86): avc:  denied  { getattr } for  pid=2427
comm="httpd" path="/var/www/html/file1" dev=dm-0 ino=284133
scontext=unconfined_u:system_r:httpd_t:s0
tcontext=unconfined_u:object_r:samba_share_t:s0 tclass=file

type=SYSCALL msg=audit(1226882736.442:86): arch=40000003 syscall=196 success=no
exit=-13 a0=b9a1e198 a1=bfc2921c a2=54dff4 a3=2008171 items=0 ppid=2425
pid=2427 auid=502 uid=48 gid=48 euid=48 suid=48 fsuid=48 egid=48 sgid=48
fsgid=48 tty=(none) ses=4 comm="httpd" exe="/usr/sbin/httpd"
subj=unconfined_u:system_r:httpd_t:s0 key=(null)
```

By default, the `httpd_t` domain is not permissive, and as such, the action is denied, and the `SYSCALL` message contains `success=no`. The following is an example AVC denial for the same situation, except the `semanage permissive -a httpd_t` command has been run to make the `httpd_t` domain permissive:

```
type=AVC msg=audit(1226882925.714:136): avc:  denied  { read } for  pid=2512
comm="httpd" name="file1" dev=dm-0 ino=284133
scontext=unconfined_u:system_r:httpd_t:s0
tcontext=unconfined_u:object_r:samba_share_t:s0 tclass=file

type=SYSCALL msg=audit(1226882925.714:136): arch=40000003 syscall=5 success=yes
exit=11 a0=b962a1e8 a1=8000 a2=0 a3=8000 items=0 ppid=2511 pid=2512 auid=502
uid=48 gid=48 euid=48 suid=48 fsuid=48 egid=48 sgid=48 fsgid=48 tty=(none)
ses=4 comm="httpd" exe="/usr/sbin/httpd" subj=unconfined_u:system_r:httpd_t:s0
key=(null)
```

In this case, although an AVC denial was logged, access was not denied, as shown by
`success=yes` in the `SYSCALL` message.

Refer to Dan Walsh's "*Permissive Domains*"[5] blog entry for further information about
permissive domains.

7.3.5. Searching For and Viewing Denials

This section assumes the setroubleshoot, setroubleshoot-server, and audit packages are
installed, and that the `auditd`, `rsyslogd`, and `setroubleshootd` daemons are running.
Refer to *Section 5.2, "Which Log File is Used"* for information about starting these daemons. A
number of tools are available for searching for and viewing SELinux denials, such as
`ausearch`, `aureport`, and `sealert`.

ausearch

The audit package provides `ausearch`. From the ausearch(8) manual page: "ausearch is a
tool that can query the audit daemon logs based for events based on different search
criteria"[6]. The `ausearch` tool accesses `/var/log/audit/audit.log`, and as such, must be
run as the Linux root user:

Searching For	Command
all denials	`/sbin/ausearch -m avc`
denials for that today	`/sbin/ausearch -m avc -ts today`
denials from the last 10 minutes	`/sbin/ausearch -m avc -ts recent`

To search for SELinux denials for a particular service, use the `-c comm-name` option, where
`comm-name` "is the executable's name"[7], for example, `httpd` for the Apache HTTP Server, and
`smbd` for Samba:

```
/sbin/ausearch -m avc -c httpd
/sbin/ausearch -m avc -c smbd
```

Refer to the ausearch(8) manual page for further `ausearch` options.

---

[5] *http://danwalsh.livejournal.com/24537.html*
[6] From the ausearch(8) manual page, as shipped with the audit package in Fedora 11.
[7] From the ausearch(8) manual page, as shipped with the audit package in Fedora 11.

aureport

The audit package provides `aureport`. From the aureport(8) manual page: "`aureport` is a tool that produces summary reports of the audit system logs"[8]. The `aureport` tool accesses `/var/log/audit/audit.log`, and as such, must be run as the Linux root user. To view a list of SELinux denials and how often each one occurred, run the `aureport -a` command. The following is example output that includes two denials:

```
# /sbin/aureport -a

AVC Report
======================================================================
# date time comm subj syscall class permission obj event
======================================================================
1. 05/01/2009 21:41:39 httpd unconfined_u:system_r:httpd_t:s0 195 file getattr
system_u:object_r:samba_share_t:s0 denied 2
2. 05/03/2009 22:00:25 vsftpd unconfined_u:system_r:ftpd_t:s0 5 file read
unconfined_u:object_r:cifs_t:s0 denied 4
```

Refer to the aureport(8) manual page for further `aureport` options.

sealert

The setroubleshoot-server package provides `sealert`, which reads denial messages translated by setroubleshoot-server. Denials are assigned IDs, as seen in `/var/log/messages`. The following is an example denial from `messages`:

```
setroubleshoot: SELinux is preventing httpd (httpd_t) "getattr" to
/var/www/html/file1 (samba_share_t). For complete SELinux messages. run sealert
-l 84e0b04d-d0ad-4347-8317-22e74f6cd020
```

In this example, the denial ID is `84e0b04d-d0ad-4347-8317-22e74f6cd020`. The `-l` option takes an ID as an argument. Running the `sealert -l 84e0b04d-d0ad-4347-8317-22e74f6cd020` command presents a detailed analysis of why SELinux denied access, and a possible solution for allowing access.

If you are running the X Window System, have the setroubleshoot and setroubleshoot-server packages installed, and the `setroubleshootd` and `auditd` daemons are running, a yellow star and a warning are displayed when access is denied by SELinux. Clicking on the star launches the `sealert` GUI, and displays denials in HTML output:

---

[8] From the aureport(8) manual page, as shipped with the audit package in Fedora 11.

The following is a reproduction of a GUI alert browser window:

Quiet	Date		Host	Count	Category	Summary
■	Wed 05 Nov 2008 06:53:05 PM EST	^	rawhide	2	File Label	SELinux is preventing httpd (h

Summary

SELinux is preventing httpd (httpd_t) "getattr" to /var/www/html/file1 (samba_share_t).

Detailed Description

SELinux denied access to /var/www/html/file1 requested by httpd. /var/www/html/file1 has a context used for sharing by different program. If you would like to share /var/www/html/file1 from httpd also, you need to change its file context to public_content_t. If you did not intend to this access, this could signal a intrusion attempt.

Allowing Access

You can alter the file context by executing chcon -t public_content_t '/var/www/html/file1'

Fix Command

chcon -t public_content_t '/var/www/html/file1'

Additional Information

Source Context:	unconfined_u:system_r:httpd_t:s0
Target Context:	unconfined_u:object_r:samba_share_t:s0
Target Objects:	/var/www/html/file1 [file]
Source:	httpd
Source Path:	/usr/sbin/httpd
Port:	<Unknown>
Host:	rawhide
Source RPM Packages:	httpd-2.2.10-2

- Run the `sealert -b` command to launch the `sealert` GUI.

- Run the `sealert -l *` command to view a detailed analysis of all denials.

- As the Linux root user, run the `sealert -a /var/log/audit/audit.log -H > audit.html` command to create a HTML version of the `sealert` analysis, as seen with the `sealert` GUI.

Refer to the sealert(8) manual page for further `sealert` options.

7.3.6. Raw Audit Messages

Raw audit messages are logged to `/var/log/audit/audit.log`. The following is an example AVC denial (and the associated system call) that occurred when the Apache HTTP Server (running in the `httpd_t` domain) attempted to access the `/var/www/html/file1` file (labeled with the `samba_share_t` type):

```
type=AVC msg=audit(1226874073.147:96): avc:  denied  { getattr } for  pid=2465
comm="httpd" path="/var/www/html/file1" dev=dm-0 ino=284133
scontext=unconfined_u:system_r:httpd_t:s0
tcontext=unconfined_u:object_r:samba_share_t:s0 tclass=file
```

```
type=SYSCALL msg=audit(1226874073.147:96): arch=40000003 syscall=196 success=no
exit=-13 a0=b98df198 a1=bfec85dc a2=54dff4 a3=2008171 items=0 ppid=2463
pid=2465 auid=502 uid=48 gid=48 euid=48 suid=48 fsuid=48 egid=48 sgid=48
fsgid=48 tty=(none) ses=6 comm="httpd" exe="/usr/sbin/httpd"
subj=unconfined_u:system_r:httpd_t:s0 key=(null)
```

{ getattr }

The item in braces indicates the permission that was denied. `getattr` indicates the source process was trying to read the target file's status information. This occurs before reading files. This action is denied due to the file being accessed having the wrong label. Commonly seen permissions include `getattr`, `read`, and `write`.

comm=*"httpd"*

The executable that launched the process. The full path of the executable is found in the `exe=` section of the system call (`SYSCALL`) message, which in this case, is `exe="/usr/sbin/httpd"`.

path=*"/var/www/html/file1"*

The path to the object (target) the process attempted to access.

scontext=*"unconfined_u:system_r:httpd_t:s0"*

The SELinux context of the process that attempted the denied action. In this case, it is the SELinux context of the Apache HTTP Server, which is running in the `httpd_t` domain.

tcontext=*"unconfined_u:object_r:samba_share_t:s0"*

The SELinux context of the object (target) the process attempted to access. In this case, it is the SELinux context of `file1`. Note: the `samba_share_t` type is not accessible to processes running in the `httpd_t` domain.

In certain situations, the `tcontext` may match the `scontext`, for example, when a process attempts to execute a system service that will change characteristics of that running process, such as the user ID. Also, the `tcontext` may match the `scontext` when a process tries to use more resources (such as memory) than normal limits allow, resulting in a security check to see if that process is allowed to break those limits.

From the system call (`SYSCALL`) message, two items are of interest:

- `success=no`: indicates whether the denial (AVC) was enforced or not. `success=no` indicates the system call was not successful (SELinux denied access). `success=yes` indicates the system call was successful - this can be seen for permissive domains or unconfined domains, such as `initrc_t` and `kernel_t`.

- `exe="/usr/sbin/httpd"`: the full path to the executable that launched the process, which in this case, is `exe="/usr/sbin/httpd"`.

An incorrect file type is a common cause for SELinux denying access. To start troubleshooting, compare the source context (`scontext`) with the target context (`tcontext`). Should the process (`scontext`) be accessing such an object (`tcontext`)? For example, the Apache HTTP Server (`httpd_t`) should only be accessing types specified in the httpd_selinux(8) manual page, such as `httpd_sys_content_t`, `public_content_t`, and so on, unless configured otherwise.

7.3.7. sealert Messages

Denials are assigned IDs, as seen in `/var/log/messages`. The following is an example AVC denial (logged to `messages`) that occurred when the Apache HTTP Server (running in the `httpd_t` domain) attempted to access the `/var/www/html/file1` file (labeled with the `samba_share_t` type):

```
hostname setroubleshoot: SELinux is preventing httpd (httpd_t) "getattr" to
/var/www/html/file1 (samba_share_t). For complete SELinux messages. run sealert
-l 84e0b04d-d0ad-4347-8317-22e74f6cd020
```

As suggested, run the `sealert -l 84e0b04d-d0ad-4347-8317-22e74f6cd020` command to view the complete message. This command only works on the local machine, and presents the same information as the `sealert` GUI:

```
$ sealert -l 84e0b04d-d0ad-4347-8317-22e74f6cd020

Summary:

SELinux is preventing httpd (httpd_t) "getattr" to /var/www/html/file1
(samba_share_t).

Detailed Description:

SELinux denied access to /var/www/html/file1 requested by httpd.
/var/www/html/file1 has a context used for sharing by different program. If you
would like to share /var/www/html/file1 from httpd also, you need to change its
file context to public_content_t. If you did not intend to this access, this
could signal a intrusion attempt.

Allowing Access:

You can alter the file context by executing chcon -t public_content_t
'/var/www/html/file1'

Fix Command:

chcon -t public_content_t '/var/www/html/file1'

Additional Information:

Source Context                   unconfined_u:system_r:httpd_t:s0
```

```
Target Context              unconfined_u:object_r:samba_share_t:s0
Target Objects              /var/www/html/file1 [ file ]
Source                      httpd
Source Path                 /usr/sbin/httpd
Port                        <Unknown>
Host                        hostname
Source RPM Packages         httpd-2.2.10-2
Target RPM Packages
Policy RPM                  selinux-policy-3.5.13-11.fc11
Selinux Enabled             True
Policy Type                 targeted
MLS Enabled                 True
Enforcing Mode              Enforcing
Plugin Name                 public_content
Host Name                   hostname
Platform                    Linux hostname 2.6.27.4-68.fc11.i686 #1 SMP
Thu Oct
30 00:49:42 EDT 2008 i686 i686
Alert Count                 4
First Seen                  Wed Nov  5 18:53:05 2008
Last Seen                   Wed Nov  5 01:22:58 2008
Local ID                    84e0b04d-d0ad-4347-8317-22e74f6cd020
Line Numbers

Raw Audit Messages

node=hostname type=AVC msg=audit(1225812178.788:101): avc:  denied  { getattr }
for  pid=2441 comm="httpd" path="/var/www/html/file1" dev=dm-0 ino=284916
scontext=unconfined_u:system_r:httpd_t:s0
tcontext=unconfined_u:object_r:samba_share_t:s0 tclass=file

node=hostname type=SYSCALL msg=audit(1225812178.788:101): arch=40000003
syscall=196 success=no exit=-13 a0=b8e97188 a1=bf87aaac a2=54dff4 a3=2008171
items=0 ppid=2439 pid=2441 auid=502 uid=48 gid=48 euid=48 suid=48 fsuid=48
egid=48 sgid=48 fsgid=48 tty=(none) ses=3 comm="httpd" exe="/usr/sbin/httpd"
subj=unconfined_u:system_r:httpd_t:s0 key=(null)
```

Summary

A brief summary of the denied action. This is the same as the denial in
/var/log/messages. In this example, the httpd process was denied access to a file
(file1), which is labeled with the samba_share_t type.

Detailed Description

A more verbose description. In this example, file1 is labeled with the samba_share_t
type. This type is used for files and directories that you want to export via Samba. The
description suggests changing the type to a type that can be accessed by the Apache
HTTP Server and Samba, if such access is desired.

Allowing Access

A suggestion for how to allow access. This may be relabeling files, turning a Boolean on, or making a local policy module. In this case, the suggestion is to label the file with a type accessible to both the Apache HTTP Server and Samba.

Fix Command

A suggested command to allow access and resolve the denial. In this example, it gives the command to change the `file1` type to `public_content_t`, which is accessible to the Apache HTTP Server and Samba.

Additional Information

Information that is useful in bug reports, such as the policy package name and version (`selinux-policy-3.5.13-11.fc11`), but may not help towards solving why the denial occurred.

Raw Audit Messages

The raw audit messages from `/var/log/audit/audit.log` that are associated with the denial. Refer to *Section 7.3.6, "Raw Audit Messages"* for information about each item in the AVC denial.

7.3.8. Allowing Access: audit2allow

Do not use the example in this section in production. It is used only to demonstrate the use of `audit2allow`.

From the audit2allow(1) manual page: "`audit2allow` - generate SELinux policy allow rules from logs of denied operations"[9]. After analyzing denials as per *Section 7.3.7, "sealert Messages"*, and if no label changes or Booleans allowed access, use `audit2allow` to create a local policy module. After access is denied by SELinux, running the `audit2allow` command presents Type Enforcement rules that allow the previously denied access.

The following example demonstrates using `audit2allow` to create a policy module:

1. A denial and the associated system call are logged to `/var/log/audit/audit.log`:

    ```
    type=AVC msg=audit(1226270358.848:238): avc:  denied  { write } for
    pid=13349 comm="certwatch" name="cache" dev=dm-0 ino=218171
    scontext=system_u:system_r:certwatch_t:s0
    tcontext=system_u:object_r:var_t:s0 tclass=dir
    ```

---

[9] From the audit2allow(1) manual page, as shipped with the policycoreutils package in Fedora 11.

```
type=SYSCALL msg=audit(1226270358.848:238): arch=40000003 syscall=39
success=no exit=-13 a0=39a2bf a1=3ff a2=3a0354 a3=94703c8 items=0 ppid=13344
pid=13349 auid=4294967295 uid=0 gid=0 euid=0 suid=0 fsuid=0 egid=0 sgid=0
fsgid=0 tty=(none) ses=4294967295 comm="certwatch" exe="/usr/bin/certwatch"
subj=system_u:system_r:certwatch_t:s0 key=(null)
```

In this example, **certwatch** (`comm="certwatch"`) was denied write access (`{ write }`) to a directory labeled with the `var_t` type (`tcontext=system_u:object_r:var_t:s0`). Analyze the denial as per *Section 7.3.7, "sealert Messages"*. If no label changes or Booleans allowed access, use `audit2allow` to create a local policy module.

2. With a denial logged, such as the `certwatch` denial in step 1, run the `audit2allow -w -a` command to produce a human-readable description of why access was denied. The `-a` option causes all audit logs to be read. The `-w` option produces the human-readable description. The `audit2allow` tool accesses `/var/log/audit/audit.log`, and as such, must be run as the Linux root user:

```
# audit2allow -w -a
type=AVC msg=audit(1226270358.848:238): avc:  denied  { write } for
pid=13349 comm="certwatch" name="cache" dev=dm-0 ino=218171
scontext=system_u:system_r:certwatch_t:s0
tcontext=system_u:object_r:var_t:s0 tclass=dir
        Was caused by:
             Missing type enforcement (TE) allow rule.

        You can use audit2allow to generate a loadable module to allow this
access.
```

As shown, access was denied due to a missing Type Enforcement rule.

3. Run the `audit2allow -a` command to view the Type Enforcement rule that allows the denied access:

```
# audit2allow -a


#============= certwatch_t ==============
allow certwatch_t var_t:dir write;
```

Important

Missing Type Enforcement rules are usually caused by bugs in SELinux policy, and should be reported in *Red Hat Bugzilla*[10]. For Fedora, create bugs against the `Fedora` product, and select the `selinux-policy` component. Include the output of the `audit2allow -w -a` and `audit2allow -a` commands in such bug reports.

---

[10] *https://bugzilla.redhat.com/*

4. To use the rule displayed by `audit2allow -a`, run the `audit2allow -a -M mycertwatch` command as the Linux root user to create custom module. The `-M` option creates a Type Enforcement file (`.te`) with the name specified with `-M`, in your current working directory:

```
# audit2allow -a -M mycertwatch


******************** IMPORTANT ***********************
To make this policy package active, execute:

semodule -i mycertwatch.pp

# ls
mycertwatch.pp  mycertwatch.te
```

Also, `audit2allow` compiles the Type Enforcement rule into a policy package (`.pp`). To install the module, run the `/usr/sbin/semodule -i mycertwatch.pp` command as the Linux root user.

 **Important**

Modules created with `audit2allow` may allow more access than required. It is recommended that policy created with `audit2allow` be posted to an SELinux list, such as *fedora-selinux-list*[11], for review. If you believe their is a bug in policy, create a bug in *Red Hat Bugzilla*[12].

If you have multiple denials from multiple processes, but only want to create a custom policy for a single process, use the `grep` command to narrow down the input for `audit2allow`. The following example demonstrates using `grep` to only send denials related to `certwatch` through `audit2allow`:

```
# grep certwatch /var/log/audit/audit.log | audit2allow -M mycertwatch2
******************** IMPORTANT ***********************
To make this policy package active, execute:

# /usr/sbin/semodule -i mycertwatch2.pp
```

Refer to Dan Walsh's "*Using audit2allow to build policy modules. Revisited.*"[13] blog entry for further information about using `audit2allow` to build policy modules.

---

[11] *http://www.redhat.com/mailman/listinfo/fedora-selinux-list*
[12] *htttps://bugzilla.redhat.com/*
[13] *http://danwalsh.livejournal.com/24750.html*

Chapter 8.
Further Information

The National Security Agency (NSA)

From the NSA *Contributors to SELinux*[1] page:

Researchers in NSA's National Information Assurance Research Laboratory (NIARL) designed and implemented flexible mandatory access controls in the major subsystems of the Linux kernel and implemented the new operating system components provided by the Flask architecture, namely the security server and the access vector cache. The NSA researchers reworked the LSM-based SELinux for inclusion in Linux 2.6. NSA has also led the development of similar controls for the X Window System (XACE/XSELinux) and for Xen (XSM/Flask).

- Main SELinux website: *http://www.nsa.gov/research/selinux/index.shtml*.
- SELinux documentation: *http://www.nsa.gov/research/selinux/docs.shtml*.
- SELinux background: *http://www.nsa.gov/research/selinux/background.shtml*.

Tresys Technology

Tresys Technology[2] are the upstream for:

- *SELinux userland libraries and tools*[3].
- *SELinux Reference Policy*[4].

SELinux News

- News: *http://selinuxnews.org/wp/*.
- Planet SELinux (blogs): *http://selinuxnews.org/planet/*.

SELinux Project Wiki

- Main page: *http://selinuxproject.org/page/Main_Page*.
- User resources, including links to documentation, mailing lists, websites, and tools: *http://selinuxproject.org/page/User_Resources*.

---

[1] *http://www.nsa.gov/research/selinux/contrib.shtml*

[2] *http://www.tresys.com/*

[3] *http://userspace.selinuxproject.org/trac/*

[4] *http://oss.tresys.com/projects/refpolicy*

Red Hat Enterprise Linux

- The *Red Hat Enterprise Linux Deployment Guide*[5] contains an SELinux *References*[6] section, that has links to SELinux tutorials, general information, and the technology behind SELinux.
- The *Red Hat Enterprise Linux 4 SELinux Guide*[7].

Fedora

- Main page: *http://fedoraproject.org/wiki/SELinux*.
- Troubleshooting: *http://fedoraproject.org/wiki/SELinux/Troubleshooting*.
- Fedora Core 5 SELinux FAQ: *http://docs.fedoraproject.org/selinux-faq-fc5/*.

The UnOfficial SELinux FAQ

http://www.crypt.gen.nz/selinux/faq.html

IRC

On *Freenode*[8]:

- #selinux
- #fedora-selinux

---

[5] *http://www.redhat.com/docs/en-US/Red_Hat_Enterprise_Linux/5.2/html/Deployment_Guide/index.html*
[6] *http://www.redhat.com/docs/en-US/Red_Hat_Enterprise_Linux/5.2/html/Deployment_Guide/selg-chapter-0054.html*
[7] *http://www.redhat.com/docs/manuals/enterprise/RHEL-4-Manual/selinux-guide/index.html*
[8] *http://freenode.net/*

Revision History

Revision History	Data	Author
Revision 1.3 Revision for Fedora 11	Tue May 12 2009	Scott Radvan
Revision 1.2 Updating hyperlinks to NSA websites	Mon Jan 19 2009	Murray McAllister
Revision 1.1 Resolving *Red Hat Bugzilla #472986,* *"httpd does not write to /etc/httpd/logs/"*[1] Added new section, "6.6. Booleans for Users Executing Applications". Minor text revisions	Sat Dec 6 2008	Murray McAllister
Revision 1.0 Initial content release on *http://docs.fedoraproject.org/*	Tue Nov 25 2008	Murray McAllister

---

[1] *https://bugzilla.redhat.com/show_bug.cgi?id=472986*

LaVergne, TN USA
12 December 2009
166739LV00006B/29/P

9 781596 821453